Distr.
GENERAL
E/ESCWA/EAD/2005/3
7 January 2005
ORIGINAL: ENGLISH

ECONOMIC AND SOCIAL COMMISSION FOR WESTERN ASIA

ANALYSIS OF PERFORMANCE AND ASSESSMENT OF GROWTH AND PRODUCTIVITY IN THE ESCWA REGION

Third Issue

United Nations
New York, 2005

E/ESCWA/EAD/2005/3
ISSN 1727-5857
ISBN 92-1-128282-9
05-0025

UNITED NATIONS PUBLICATION
Sales No. E.05.II.L.7

Per

UNI

E/ESCWA

A56

CONTENTS

Page

Executive summary v
Introduction 1

Chapter

  I. THE INVESTMENT CLIMATE IN THE ESCWA REGION 2

    A. No clear responsiveness of gross fixed capital formation to savings
       in the ESCWA region 2

    B. Weak responsiveness of GDP per capita growth to investment rates
       in the ESCWA region 3

    C. Description of trends in the investment climate of the ESCWA region 3

 II. DEMAND AND SUPPLY SIDE CHARACTERISTICS OF SAVINGS
    AND INVESTMENT 8

    A. Demand side characteristics 8
    B. Supply side characteristics 13

III. EMPIRICAL INVESTIGATION OF THE DETERMINANTS OF
    INVESTMENT CLIMATES 18

    A. Methodology 18
    B. Empirical results 18

IV. POLICY RECOMMENDATIONS 20

LIST OF FIGURES

1. Responsiveness of investment to savings in developing regions and
   in the ESCWA region 2

2. Responsiveness of investment rates to savings rates in oil-exporting economies 3

3. Responsiveness of investment rates to savings rates in the more diversified economies 3

4. Responsiveness of GDP per capita growth in developing regions and
   in the ESCWA region 4

5. Responsiveness of GDP per capita growth rates to investment rates in
   oil-exporting economies 4

6. Responsiveness of GDP per capita growth rates to investment rates
   in the more diversified economies 4

7. Stylized methodology of identifying investment climates 5

8. Market size and savings rates 8

9. Market size and investment rates 8

10. Purchasing power and savings rates 9

11. Purchasing power and investment rates 9

12. Growth volatility and savings rates in the whole sample and in the ESCWA region 10

13. Growth volatility and investment rates in the whole sample and in the ESCWA region 10

CONTENTS (*continued*)

Page

14. Growth volatility and savings rates in the oil-exporting economies 10
15. Growth volatility and investment rates in the oil-exporting economies 10
16. Growth volatility and savings rates in the more diversified economies 10
17. Growth volatility and investment rates in the more diversified economies 10
18. Savings and country risk 11
19. Investment and country risk 11
20. Savings and debt 11
21. Investment and debt 11
22. Savings' rates and government consumption 12
23. Investment rates and government consumption 12
24. Savings and foreign trade share 14
25. Investment and foreign trade share 14
26. Savings and manufacturing 14
27. Investment and manufacturing 14
28. Savings and GDP share of manufactured goods without fuel exports 14
29. Investment and GDP share of manufactured goods without fuel exports 14
30. Savings and market capitalization 15
31. Investment and market capitalization 15
32. Savings and secondary school enrolment 16
33. Investment and secondary school enrolment 16
34. Savings and income inequality 16
45. Investment and income inequality 16

ANNEXES

  I. Country list 21
 II. Variable list and technical details 22
III. Country tables 24

Executive Summary

This report examines recent developments in the resource mobilization climate in the Economic and Social Commission for Western Asia (ESCWA) region and compares them to trends related to a wider sample of developing countries. The results are reviewed below.

While it may be the case that oil economies are characterized by a higher responsiveness of investment to savings rates than more diversified economies, this can perhaps be wholly attributed to oil rent windfall. Moreover, while the responsiveness of investment to savings in the diversified economies is lower, higher investment rates translate into higher per capita growth rates than in the oil economies. Oil economies are regularly identified as resource exporters, which are characterized by high saving rates accompanied by low investment rates, and diversified economies as resource importers or vicious cyclists, meaning they have high or low investment rates related to low saving rates.

The oil economies have experienced, on average, a continuous deterioration of their investment climate. Moreover, great vulnerability to oil price fluctuations continues to characterize the oil economies, which were super investors, with high savings and high investment, in the 1970s and 1980s and became resource exporters in the 1990s.

The resource mobilization dynamics in the more diversified region are not uniform. For example, Egypt experienced a severe deterioration and the Syrian Arab Republic a real improvement of their investment climates during the 1990s. Standard growth theory does not wholly apply to economies that are either built on oil, or trapped in social and political turmoil. Indeed, the risk component is a major contributor to poor growth in the ESCWA region.

In order to understand the investment climate in the ESCWA region more fully, determinants of savings and gross fixed capital formation are explored from various demand and supply side angles.

On the demand side, larger regional markets have the potential of inducing a higher savings rate; it must be noted, however, that investment rates in the ESCWA region may be lower than in other regions, which seems to indicate that a huge investment opportunity is being lost as a result of the absence of intraregional market expansion in the region. Greater regional domestic markets are generally rich in resources and enjoy a significant windfall from oil rents. Moreover, purchasing power reconfirms the positive relationship with savings rates; regionally, however, this exhibits a weak relationship with gross fixed capital formation, demonstrating the distorting impact of leakages and strong intraregional inequalities.

Another obstacle to a favourable investment climate in the ESCWA region lies in market risk. Country risk is a major deterrent for both savings and the formation of capital stock. While the ESCWA region made substantial progress in reducing country risk in the 1980s and 1990s, recent conflicts are likely to harm the investment climate in the region.

Overall debt and debt overhang exhibit a negative relationship with savings, particularly in the case of the diversified economies.

Savings rates respond less to government consumption in the ESCWA region than they do in developing countries according to the average for those countries. Moreover, the diversified economies exhibit small and declining government shares. Empirical evidence suggests that the decline has been unfavourable in terms of investment and development, based on the fact that there is a need for public investment in physical and institutional infrastructure in the ESCWA region.

According to the empirical investigation, there is a strong positive correlation between foreign trade share and investment rates, which is a matter that can be easily relegated to windfall oil earnings. Non-oil trade activity in the ESCWA region is among the lowest in the developing world. While the oil subregion has a comparatively high trade share, it can be noted that after controlling for per capita income and fuel exports, this becomes very small.

The role of manufacturing in savings and investment highlights the weak contribution of this sector to the development of the ESCWA region. As a corollary to this, developed capital markets are also identified as favourable to savings and investment rates.

Furthermore, high levels of educational attainment enhance the investment climate of a country. While numbers indicate, on average, an improvement in enrolment rates in the ESCWA region, the quality of educational attainment is still comparatively low as regards favouring a better investment environment.

It can also be noted that income inequality in the ESCWA region reduces the rate of growth of gross fixed capital formation. The ESCWA region has one of the highest income inequalities in the world, which serves as a major obstacle to the investment atmosphere.

Empirical analysis therefore demonstrates that small markets, low purchasing power, high growth volatility, high country risk, low trade shares, a small manufacturing base and high inequality of income represent major obstacles for economic development in the ESCWA region.

The region requires several big-push investment packages, with particular priorities being investment in plant and equipment and the improvement of the transportation infrastructure; at the same time, public education and health, and the reduction of urbanization problems are just as important. On average, the economic developmental state in the ESCWA region has a poorer success record than the developmental state in East Asia or Latin America. The greatest potential, however, is likely to arise from greater regional market dynamics. In order to accomplish this, regional trade integration must be credibly advanced in the ESCWA region. Furthermore, regional investment guarantees are necessary to revitalize the region. Unequal economic opportunities continue to suppress entrepreneurial activity. In addition to investment guarantees, the region must also provide broader access to investment opportunities, both across income groups and gender. Start-up funds and small and medium-sized enterprises' credit programmes must therefore also be initiated and ideally financed through mildly progressive taxation.

Introduction

This report represents an empirical and analytical survey of the savings and investment climate in the Economic and Social Commission for Western Asia (ESCWA) region. It does this by comparing and analysing the conditions in the ESCWA region to a larger group of developing economies. It explores the economic policy options available to policy makers with regard to enhancing economic growth and real incomes for both men and women within the framework of achieving the United Nations Millennium Development Goals.

Chapter I discusses the levels and trends of savings and investment between 1975 and 2000 in the ESCWA region, and classifies ESCWA member countries according to the following categories: super investor, resource exporter, resource importer or vicious cyclist. Super investors are characterized by high savings and high investment; resource exporters by high savings and low investment; resource importers by low savings and high investment; and vicious cyclists by low savings and low investment.

The supply and demand profile of an economy crucially determines savings and investment. Chapter II analyses this relationship. With regard to the demand side, the report investigates market size, purchasing power, gross domestic product (GDP) per capita growth volatility, country risk, central government debt and government consumption. In terms of the supply side, the report explores trade shares, size of the manufacturing sector, exports of manufactured goods, capital market development, levels of educational attainment and income inequality.

The list of characteristics affecting savings and investment can be easily expanded by such institutional factors as the efficacy of public administration, leakages, regulatory quality, transparency and improved institutional quality. Recent ESCWA research has demonstrated the relevance of institutional parameters, as they affect risk in the determination of investment, economic growth and income.[1]

Chapter III tests the empirical power of demand and supply characteristics in terms of explaining the likelihood of a country belonging to any of the four investment climates mentioned above.

Chapter IV briefly reviews national resource mobilization policies for developing countries and presents policy recommendations.

Annex I contains a list of countries in the sample in this report; variables and technical details reviewed below are defined in annex II. It is worth noting that gross fixed capital formation, or investment, and gross domestic savings are computed as five-year moving averages to smooth out erratic fluctuations. Annex III contains country tables.

All the data in this report, including data related to variables, and that have been used in the figures and tables can be attributed to the World Development Indicators (WDI) database of the World Bank Group, which is available online.

---

[1] ESCWA, *Analysis of Performances and Assessment of Growth and Productivity in the ESCWA Region*, first issue, (E/ESCWA/EAD/2003/3).

I. THE INVESTMENT CLIMATE IN THE ESCWA REGION

Economic growth and investment in the ESCWA region are highly dependent on oil revenues and strongly affected by internal and external conflicts in the region. Real per capita income has performed poorly during the past two decades. The business cycle is driven by exogenous pressures, principally, political tensions and the ensuing high level of spending on security and defence. The investment rate of the ESCWA region remains meagre despite its high rate of retained savings. Various aspects of the determinants of savings and investment are reviewed below.

A. NO CLEAR RESPONSIVENESS OF GROSS FIXED CAPITAL FORMATION TO SAVINGS IN THE ESCWA REGION

With regard to the figures below, the yellow circles and the yellow trend line represent the whole sample of developing countries, while the red triangles and red trend line represent the ESCWA region (such as figure 1). The overall trend is estimated across the developing world in East Asia and the Pacific, Latin America and the Caribbean, and the Middle East and North Africa, excluding Sub-Saharan Africa. The yellow circles that appear in those figures that do not contain red triangles represent ESCWA member countries (such as figures 2 and 3). Figures are largely based on data in the country tables in annex III, and cover the period of time detailed there.

The rate of gross fixed capital formation in the ESCWA region appears to be less responsive to gross domestic savings rates than does the trend for a greater sample of developing countries (see figure 1). This indicates a less than average performance of the intermediation between the financial sector and the real economy.

Figure 1. Responsiveness of investment to savings in developing regions and in the ESCWA region

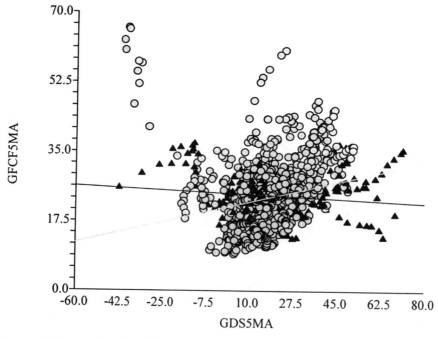

Note: Refer to annex II for an explanation of the abbreviations used.

The investment rate in the ESCWA region, across countries, was below the overall trend for the period 1975-2000, which means that savings in the ESCWA region had less potential of being translated into investment vis-à-vis the trend for the developing world for that period. It can be noted that this result can be attributed to the high rates of capital outflow from the region that have occurred since 1975.

However, when the ESCWA region is studied separately, the results vary considerably for the oil-exporting and more diversified economies (MDEs). There are two different investment climates co-existing in the ESCWA region (see figures 2 and 3). While a positive relationship between savings and investment prevails for the oil-exporting economies, such a relationship is negative for the diversified economies. The reason for the latter is that the diversified region is a mixed bag with no robust trend. For example, removing Jordan, Lebanon and the West Bank and Gaza, which all have a substantial record of negative savings rates, would restore a positive relationship between savings and investment rates for the remaining countries. Therefore, while a positive nexus of savings to investment essentially exists, it is significantly weaker than the rest of the sample.

Figure 2. Responsiveness of investment rates to savings rates in oil-exporting economies

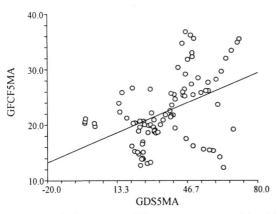

Figure 3. Responsiveness of investment rates to savings rates in the more diversified economies

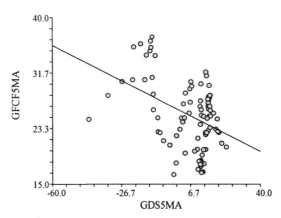

Note: Refer to annex II for an explanation of the abbreviations used.

B. WEAK RESPONSIVENESS OF GDP PER CAPITA GROWTH TO INVESTMENT
RATES IN THE ESCWA REGION

The ESCWA region exhibits different characteristics with respect to its GDP per capita growth responsiveness to investment rates (see figure 4).

The scatter plot in figure 4 suggests that per capita growth rates in the ESCWA region, as represented by the red triangles and red trend line, respond less favourably to investment rates as compared to the overall trend, which is represented by yellow dots and the yellow trend line. A separate look at the oil-exporting economies and MDEs as illustrated in the scatter plots in figures 5 and 6 shows that the GDP per capita growth rates in MDEs respond more favourably to higher investment rates than they do in the oil economies. This is because the former depend more on a more diversified physical production base than do the latter.

C. DESCRIPTION OF TRENDS IN THE INVESTMENT CLIMATE OF THE ESCWA REGION

1. *Methodology of investment climate identification*

The substantial issue of the following section refers to different investment climates, which are characterized according to the relative strengths and weaknesses of their supply and demand sides, and thereby divided into super investors, resource exporters, resource importers and vicious cyclists, which have been defined above.

Super investors are created as a result of an advantageous investment climate and generally provide the momentum for a continued rise in both saving and investment rates. On the flip side, vicious cyclists offer the least beneficial environment for the mobilization of productive resources. These are the two poles of the investment climate spectrum, with resource exporters and importers located in between.

Super investors have both a strong supply and demand side and therefore often fully finance gross fixed capital formation with domestic savings, reducing the vulnerability to external shocks. Resource exporters are also strong on the supply but weak on the demand side. Economic actors therefore opt for an export of productive resources. Conversely, resource importers are strong on the demand but weak on the supply side. Finally, vicious cyclists have both weak demand and supply sides.

Figure 4. Responsiveness of GDP per capita growth in developing regions and in the ESCWA region

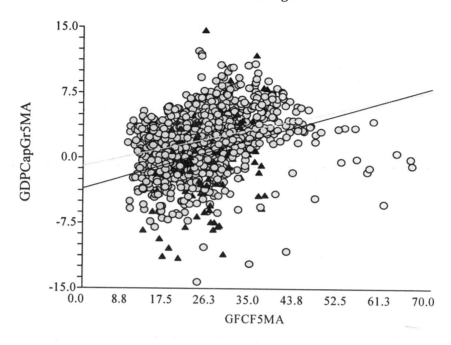

Figure 5. Responsiveness of GDP per capita growth rates to investment rates in oil-exporting economies

Figure 6. Responsiveness of GDP per capita growth rates to investment rates in the more diversified economies

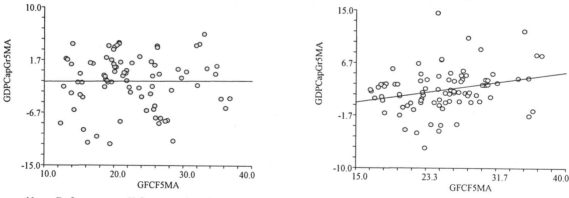

Note: Refer to annex II for an explanation of the abbreviations used.

Visually, the four investment climates can be identified in a scatter plot where savings rates on the x-axis are plotted against investment rates on the y-axis. Figure 7 stylizes such a scatter plot. Super investors are located in the green area. Super investors have above average savings rates and investment rates above the trend line. Vicious cyclists, by stark contrast, have below average savings rates and investment rates that are below the trend line. The 45-degree line shows that super investors and vicious cyclists could, in effect, be exporters or importers of resources. However, the issue that matters here with regard to the classification as super investor is simply above average savings rates and investment rates that are above the trend line. The reverse applies to vicious cyclists. While resource exporters have above average savings rates, they have investment rates that are below the trend and 45-degree line. Resource importers have below average savings rates and investment rates that are below the trend line. By computing the distance of any observation from the intersection of the 45-degree with the trend line, it is also possible to calculate the strength of each individual investment climate.

The following two sections provide an overview of the investment climate in ESCWA member countries, which are divided into oil economies and more diversified economies.

Figure 7. Stylized methodology of identifying investment climates

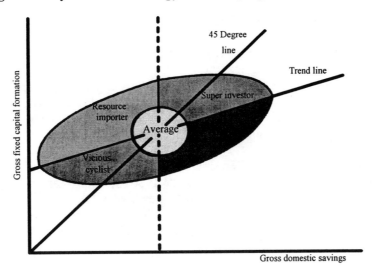

2. The investment climate and growth dynamics of the oil economies

Data on oil-exporting economies show a substantial decline in the savings/output ratio between 1975 and 1999 for most countries. Bahrain, Oman and the United Arab Emirates witnessed a continuous decline of their savings rates over time. The United Arab Emirates witnessed the sharpest decline from 76 per cent in 1975 to 36 per cent in 1992. Bahrain's savings rate went down from 50 per cent in the early 1980s to 29 per cent in 1999. Similarly, Oman's rate fell from 49 per cent in 1975 to 28 per cent in 1992. However, while Saudi Arabia and Kuwait[2] experienced a severe decline in their saving rates until the end of the 1980s, this trend later reversed slightly.

Despite the decline of the savings rate of the oil economies, they remain the biggest savers in the world. In fact, there are no observations for any oil-exporting economy except in reference to the military conflict in Kuwait when savings rate fell below the seventieth percentile rank of the sample of developing countries listed in annex I.[3]

The decrease in the savings rate must also be considered in combination with the fact that observations start during the first oil boom, most likely therefore inflating savings rates of the oil exporting economies with windfall profits. Generally, the impact of the dummy 'fuel exporter' as an explanatory variable for savings rate which is statistically and economically very significant given that it has a regression coefficient of greater than 16 percentage points. Controlling for this effect places the savings rates of most oil-exporting economies below the fortieth percentile at the end of the 1990s.

---

[2] Data pertaining to Kuwait, however, must be read with caution, as the first Gulf war appears to have accelerated the decline of its savings rate. The improvement of the savings rate after 1991 may therefore largely be attributed to the restoration of peace.

[3] Hereinafter, this ranks Kuwait to the rest of the sample of developing countries listed in annex I.

In a similar fashion to the decline of savings rates, oil-exporting economies also show a decline of investment rates, although this decline is not as severe as that of savings. Bahrain experienced the worst deterioration between 1982 and 1999, falling from 36 per cent to 13 per cent. The United Arab Emirates witnessed a decline from 36 per cent in 1977 to some 22 per cent in 1992. Saudi Arabia's level of gross fixed capital formation appeared constant at approximately 25 per cent until the mid-1980s before it began to fall slightly but continuously to 19 per cent in 1999. Lastly, Kuwait's investment rates appear constant between 15 and 20 per cent.

The decline of investment rates in the oil economies is particularly severe when compared to the rest of the developing region sample and when using percentile ranks. Bahrain, for example, fell from the ninety-third percentile rank in 1982 to the fifth percentile rank in 1999. By the end of the 1990s, Saudi Arabia ranked below the thirtieth and Kuwait below the fifth percentile rank. There are only a few observations for Oman. Those observations, however, also indicate a constant decline of investment rates.

One distinct fact of the investment climate of oil exporters is their huge excess capacity of savings to investment rates, which is mostly attributable to the monetization of wealth assets. All recent investment-climate records fall within the resource exporter cluster (see figure 7), hence high rates of gross domestic savings are associated with declining investment rates.

Consequently, GDP per capita has fallen since the 1980s. For example, 16 out of 20 observations for Saudi Arabia's GDP per capita growth rates during the 1980s and 1990s are negative. With regard to the United Arab Emirates, the ratio of observations with negative GDP per capita growth rates to total observations is 16 to 17. Kuwait's ratio is 10 to 13. Only Bahrain and Oman have weathered the trend of the other oil economies. Both economies have been on a positive GDP per capita growth path, particularly since the 1990s.

3. *The investment climate and growth dynamics of the more diversified economies*

The more diversified economies suffer chronically from low savings rates. Lebanon and the West Bank and Gaza have, exclusively, observations with negative savings rates. Jordan also exhibited negative savings rates during most of the 1980s. During the 1980s, despite having positive savings rates, Egypt and the Syrian Arab Republic regularly ranked below the fortieth percentile rank, with savings rates usually between 10 per cent and 15 per cent. Beginning in the 1990s, savings rates in Egypt declined, reaching levels of below 12 per cent in 1999, therefore placing the country below the twenty-fifth percentile rank. The Syrian Arab Republic, however, managed to increase its savings rates considerably during the 1990s, from 11 per cent in 1990 to 23 per cent in 1999, catapulting it above the seventieth percentile rank. While Jordan sustained positive savings rates during the 1990s, it has not yet managed to create double-digit savings rates. Data for Yemen shows that there was some improvement between 1992 and 1999. It increased its savings rates from negative values in 1992/93 to above 19 per cent in 1999, placing it above the fiftieth percentile.

Regarding investment rates, great volatility characterizes the diversified ESCWA region. Egypt experienced a severe decline of investment rates, starting from the end of the 1980s. While Egypt made substantial resource mobilization progress between 1975 and 1980, raising its investment rate from 19 to 28 per cent and increasing its percentile rank from 31 to 76, it found itself again at a gross fixed capital investment rate of 17 per cent and the sixteenth percentile rank in 1995.

The Syrian Arab Republic experienced a similar pattern. During the 1980s, the gross fixed capital investment ratio of the Syrian Arab Republic fell from 27 to 17 per cent, corresponding to a drop from above the seventy-fifth to below the twentieth percentile. During the 1990s, however, the Syrian Arab Republic temporarily rebounded, climbing back to a gross fixed capital formation rate of above 25 per cent in the mid 1990s. After the mid-1990s, the ratio of the Syrian Arab Republic has again been decreasing. Its investment ratio and percentile rank in 1999 were 21 per cent and thirty-seventh, respectively.

A deterioration of investment activity in the first half of the 1980s, followed by a temporary recovery until the mid-1990s and a decline thereafter again describes the situation in Jordan. Jordan had its highest gross fixed capital formation level in 1979 at 37 per cent, which placed it above the ninety-fifth percentile rank. By 1987, Jordan's investment rate fell by more than 15 percentage points to 21 per cent, corresponding to the thirty-eighth percentile rank. The following recovery reached an investment ratio of 30 per cent in 1994, placing it again above the eighty-fifth percentile rank. By 1999, Jordan's investment ratio and percentile rank again fell below 25 per cent and the sixtieth percentile rank, respectively. Despite these swings, Jordan still has the highest investment rates of all the diversified ESCWA member countries.

Given either negative or low savings rates, the investment climates of the diversified economies are hence generally classified as vicious cyclist or resource importer.

Egypt increasingly developed vicious cyclist symptoms during the 1990s. In 1991, Egypt's vicious cyclist symptoms[4] worsened from the twenty-seventh percentile rank in 1991 to the fifty-ninth percentile rank in 1999. Despite the investment and savings turmoil in Egypt, it experienced constantly positive GDP per capita growth rates over the period under consideration, principally fuelled by high levels of aid.

Compared to Egypt, GDP per capita growth rates in the Syrian Arab Republic are very volatile. However, the Syrian Arab Republic substantially increased savings and investment rates during the 1990s, making its growth prospects more favourable than has been indicated by the latest data. Jordan is among the greatest resource importers and lacks a substantial gross domestic savings base, making it consistently vulnerable to external shocks. During the 1990s, Jordan did not essentially experience any GDP per capita growth. Lebanon is also a huge importer of resources, which is mainly attributable to its post-civil war reconstruction efforts. Despite Lebanon's high investment rates during the 1990s, high GDP per capita growth rates were short-lived. Finally, while there is little data available for Yemen, its most recent data suggests a healthy investment climate in terms of savings and investment rates.

A major issue for the region is not only a non-favourable investment climate in most of the countries but also many divergent and erratic savings, investment and growth trends. The investment climate of the region would clearly benefit from a greater harmonization of economic trends, which must be accomplished through greater regional macroeconomic cooperation.

---

[4] This is measured by the distance from the intersection of the 45-degree line with the trend line of figure 7.

II. DEMAND AND SUPPLY SIDE CHARACTERISTICS
OF SAVINGS AND INVESTMENT

The following section analyses the investment climate in the region with respect to demand and supply side characteristics and compares the results to the sample group of developing countries.

A. DEMAND SIDE CHARACTERISTICS

The demand side of an economy is favourable to the investment climate in the presence of large domestic and regional markets, high per capita income, low volatility of GDP per capita growth, low country risk, sustainable debt service and smooth government consumption.

1. *Market size*

The empirical relationship between market sizes, as proxied by the natural logarithm of GDP, and savings rates suggests that large markets are favourable to higher savings propensities (see figure 8). With regard to investment rates, bigger markets tend to produce greater output with smaller investment rates, which can most likely be attributed to higher capital productivities as shown in figure 9. While the trend lines are only suggestive demarcation lines and do not imply causation, there appears to be strong support for the conclusion that large markets support a beneficial investment climate. The yellow dots and trend line again represent the whole sample; the red triangles and red trend line represent the ESCWA region.

Compared to the overall trend, irrespective of the low savings of the diversified economies, the oil economies push the average savings rate above the overall trend. With regard to the investment rate, the fragmented markets of the ESCWA region make the trend line steeper than it is for the rest of the sample. Economies at a percentile rank above 50 in the sample include Saudi Arabia, at 89; Egypt, at 82; the United Arab Emirates, at 73; Kuwait, at 65; and the Syrian Arab Republic and Lebanon, both at 55.

When the rift between oil-exporting and more diversified economies in the region is taken into account, market size appears to favour the investment climate in the oil subregion slightly more than in the MDE subregion. Broader intraregional integration therefore stimulates higher savings and encourages the accumulation of capital with greater economies of scale in the ESCWA region.

Figure 8. Market size and savings rates	Figure 9. Market size and investment rates
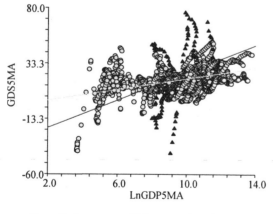	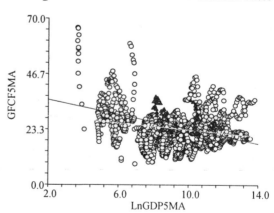

Note: Refer to annex II for an explanation of the abbreviations used.

2. *Gross domestic product per capita*

Gross domestic product per capita represents a proxy for purchasing power. The scatter plot in figure 10 shows that high per capita incomes stimulate the investment climate of an economy primarily through high savings rates. However, the scatter plot in figure 11 also suggests a slightly positive relationship between GDP per capita and domestic investment rates.

In terms of purchasing power, oil-exporting economies, of course, clearly outperform the more diversified economies. However, in terms of savings, the ESCWA region exhibits a higher average than the overall sample, which is again the result of the higher weight of the oil economies. With respect to the demand side, the ESCWA region underperforms compared to the rest of the sample, meaning that there is a lower mediation between purchasing power and investment.

All oil-exporting ESCWA economies, for which per capita income data are available, rank above the eightieth percentile rank. The economy with the highest percentile rank among the diversified economies in 1999 was Lebanon, which was at the sixty-ninth percentile rank. All other diversified economies were located far below the fiftieth percentile rank. Low purchasing power is therefore a severe handicap to the development of a favourable investment climate among the diversified economies owing to its dampening effects on the savings rate.

Figure 10. Purchasing power and savings rates   **Figure 11. Purchasing power and investment rates**

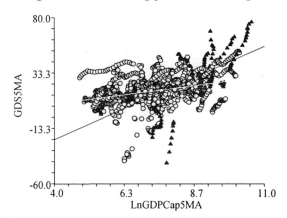
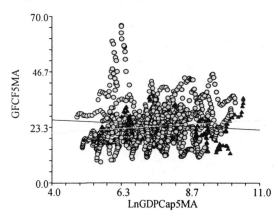

Note: Refer to annex II for an explanation of the abbreviations used.

3. *Gross domestic product per capita growth volatility*

Gross domestic product per capita growth volatility is a broad risk indicator. Figures 12 and 13 indicate no significant relationship between output growth volatility and savings rates or output growth volatility and investment rates for the whole sample. Volatility, however, is an important factor for the oil economies of the ESCWA region (see figures 14 and 15). In high-risk times, oil prices, savings and gross fixed capital formation rise; however, as oil rents recede, savings flow out and gross fixed capital formation declines. An increase in oil price raises returns on capital in the oil economies and therefore momentarily accelerates savings and investment rates. When volatility of per capita growth is investigated, the oil economies display a high vulnerability to oil price fluctuations. Periods characterized by low volatility, particularly since the 1990s, are accompanied by low oil prices and negative per capita growth rates, as is the case in Kuwait, Saudi Arabia and the United Arab Emirates, or stagnating per capita growth, as is the case in Oman.

Nevertheless, high oil prices have a dampening effect on the investment climate in MDEs (see figures 16 and 17). Volatility of per capita growth among MDEs seemed slightly more favourable during the 1990s. Egypt managed to reduce volatility of per capita growth continuously owing to the smaller size of the oil sector relative to the overall economy. Jordan also reduced per capita growth volatility during the 1990s but failed to combine it with high per capita growth. Per capita growth volatility in the Syrian Arab Republic does not show a long-run trend. Although per capita growth volatility decreased substantially and per capita growth rates were respectably high in the first half of the 1990s, the Syrian Arab Republic failed to sustain this development. Sustainable moderate to high per capita growth rates combined with little growth volatility are still rare in the ESCWA region.

Over the long run, the risk and volatility elements undermine the mobilization potential of productive resources in the ESCWA region. Greater economic diversity is necessary to forestall market risk and to increase the adjustment potential to external shocks.

Figure 12. Growth volatility and savings rates in the whole sample and in the ESCWA region

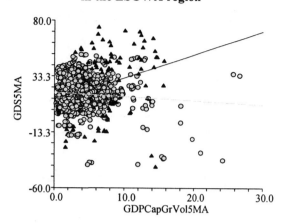

Figure 13. Growth volatility and investment rates in the whole sample and in the ESCWA region

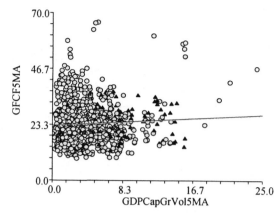

Figure 14. Growth volatility and savings rates in the oil-exporting economies

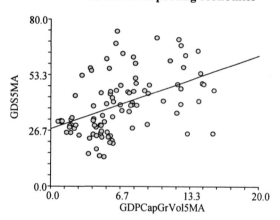

Figure 15. Growth volatility and investment rates in the oil-exporting economies

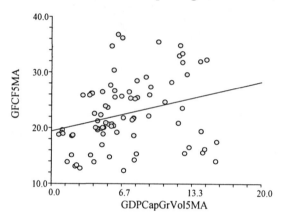

Figure 16. Growth volatility and savings rates in the more diversified economies

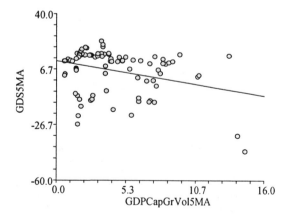

Figure 17. Growth volatility and investment rates in the more diversified economies

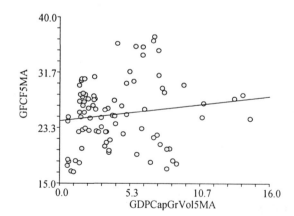

Note: Refer to annex II for an explanation of the abbreviations used.

4. *Country risk*

Growth volatility is closely related to the overall exposure to political instability, civil upheaval and military conflict of a country. The International Country Risk Guide index, which is used here, attempts to capture country risk. The scatter plots in figures 18 and 19 show that little country risk (higher index values) tends to stimulate savings and investment rates. While the ESCWA region is well aligned with the overall trend in terms of savings rates, it is not aligned with the overall trend in terms of investment rates. This means that in the ESCWA region lower country risk is associated with smaller investment rates. While the oil economies in the region generally have lower country risk than the more diversified economies, their investment rates trend to be lower. During the period under consideration, the risk levels were high or quite high, draining the potential for an effective transfer of savings into investment.

Figure 18. Savings and country risk

GDS5MA vs ICRG5MA

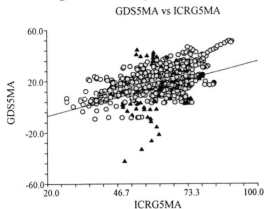

Figure 19. Investment and country risk

GFCF5MA vs ICRG5MA

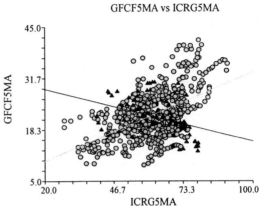

5. *Debt*

Debt is another important factor that affects the investment climate of an economy from the demand side, based on the fact that unsustainable governmental debt creates a fiscal drag that leads to a poor growth performance. In figures 20 and 21, higher indebtedness in the ESCWA region is associated with a lower comparative savings rate and a higher investment rate. The former condition denotes that the region experiences a significant resource leakage, hence reducing effective private or public savings.[5] Capital inflows (rent or otherwise) are channelled into raising consumption. Additionally, rising foreign imports reduced savings by stimulating the consumption of both importable and exportable components of the regional economy. The biggest crunch on domestic savings, however, remains that of insecurity and less substantively, the underdeveloped state of the financial market.

Despite the fact that debt is high in the ESCWA region, debt service need not be an issue in the sense that some States are capable of restructuring this factor through moderate progressive taxation and can thus make debt more sustainable and less of a drag on the economy.

Figure 20. Savings and debt

GDS5MA vs Debt5MA

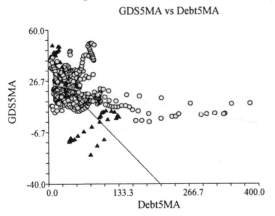

Figure 21. Investment and debt

GFCF5MA vs Debt5MA

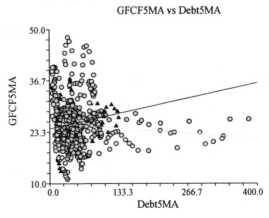

Note: Refer to annex II for an explanation of the abbreviations used.

---

[5] Effective savings are retained domestic savings excluding savings held by nationals of the region abroad. The latter cannot be factored into domestic savings because, under the prevalent conditions of tensions and market structures, it is unlikely that these savings will ever be repatriated. It may be difficult to speak of excess savings when the growth rate is, on average, low.

6. *Government consumption*

Government consumption in the ESCWA region displays a stronger relationship with savings than it does in the rest of the sample and a weaker one with investment (see figures 22 and 23). Public consumption can in effect improve infrastructure, education, health services and the efficiency of public administration. It can also divert resources to law and order activities. However, this is not necessarily the case in the ESCWA region, where the return on one dollar spent on social investment is usually small. This is more pronounced for the oil-exporting States where final government consumption of GDP is quite high and disguised unemployment is rampant in Government.

Government consumption in Oman, for which the last observation was 1992, accounted for more than 33 per cent of GDP. Other oil economies still rank above the sixtieth percentile. More diversified economies again provided a mixed bag. In 1999, Jordan had the highest share of government consumption, at over 23 per cent and with a percentile rank of 87; followed by Lebanon, with 15 per cent and percentile rank of 52; and Egypt and the Syrian Arab Republic, both with some 11 per cent and a percentile rank of approximately 30. Egypt, Jordan and Syrian Arab Republic are furthermore characterized by a severe decline of government consumption over the past two decades. While low government consumption can at times be considered beneficial to growth, empirical evidence does not support this conclusion in the case of the ESCWA region. Therefore, the relationship between governmental consumption and resource mobilization is dependant on retargeting and improving the quality of government consumption or the return on social investment.

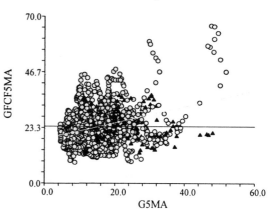

Figure 22. Savings rates and government consumption

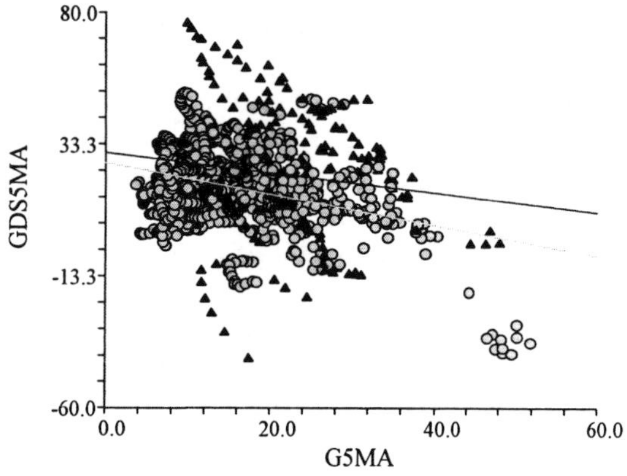

Figure 23. Investment rates and government consumption

Note: Refer to annex II for an explanation of the abbreviations used.

7. *Summary of demand side characteristics*

Aggregate demand and purchasing power are essential prerequisites for the accumulation of capital in the ESCWA region. Volatility of GDP per capita growth tends to be rather hampering in terms of regional economic performance. Moreover, while data for overall country risk shows a general reduction of risk during the 1990s, the risk level in the ESCWA region continues to be too high, and the poor performance of investment and savings is likely to persist. Central government debt is more of a concern for MDEs because of their lower wealth profile. Government consumption among MDEs has fallen to low levels and may have adversely affected economic growth by depressing aggregate demand. It can be noted that economic development substantially depends on public complements to private production factors. The level of institutional development does not allow high government consumption in the oil economies to translate into high per capita growth.

The analysis above therefore suggests that the major obstacles in the ESCWA region to the mobilization of productive resources on the demand side stem from small markets, high volatility, low purchasing power and high risk.

B. Supply side characteristics

The supply side of an economy is favourable to the investment climate in the presence of high trade shares, a broad manufacturing base, access to capital markets, a well-educated labour force, and equal economic opportunities for men and women.

1. *Trade shares*

Intraregional openness of an economy is crucial in that it permits a vent-for-surplus of production and therefore the realization of economies of scale, in addition to the importation of knowledge and ideas. The scatter plots in figures 24 and 25 show that the foreign trade share of an economy improves its investment climate through an increase of the gross fixed capital formation and savings rates.

In the ESCWA region, fuel-exporting economies exhibit high trade shares. The graphical illustration below indicates that higher trade shares are associated with higher savings in the ESCWA region relative to the rest of the sample. Nevertheless, the ESCWA region performs below the trend with respect to investment rates, which can be attributed to heavy capital outflows and consumption leakages.

Saudi Arabia's trend is particularly dramatic. Its trade share fell from approximately 100 per cent of GDP in 1980 to 63 per cent in 1999. This corresponds to a decline from above the seventieth percentile to below the forty-fifth percentile rank. The percentile ranks of Kuwait and Oman also reduced during the 1980s and 1990s.

All oil economies have foreign trade shares below the trend line of the sample when controlling for per capita income. With regard to Saudi Arabia, this means that the actual decrease in percentile rank is from above 45 to below 15. When controlling for per capita income, Kuwait's foreign trade share ranks far below the thirtieth percentile rank. The United Arab Emirates is the only country that seems to withstand the declining regional trade share trend when controlling for per capita income, which may in part be explained by the diversified trade portfolio of Dubai.

A similar result can be witnessed in the case of the GDP share of exported manufactured goods. Without controlling for fuel exports, export shares of all the oil economies are above the seventy-fifth percentile rank. After controlling for fuel exports, Kuwait and Saudi Arabia are below the tenth percentile rank. Oman also experienced a substantial drop of its percentile rank from above 95 in 1982 to below 40 in 1998. The United Arab Emirates is the only economy that weathered the trend, showing it has a more diversified trade portfolio than other countries in the oil region.

The picture of MDEs is again not uniform. The trade share of Egypt has behaved very erratically with a clear downward trend during the 1990s. In 1990, Egypt's trade share was still 56 per cent of GDP and fell to below 42 per cent in 1999. This corresponds to a decrease of its percentile rank from 38 to 22. The trade share of Lebanon, not including trade in services, also constantly fell during the 1990s. Jordan and the Syrian Arab Republic have greater trade shares relative to the rest. When controlled for per capita income, Jordan and the Syrian Arab Republic trade at levels even greater than the trend. The Syrian Arab Republic in particular, appears to have made notable intraregional trade liberalization progress during the 1990s.

2. *Manufacturing*

The development of a broad and competitive manufacturing base is crucial for the investment climate of a country for many reasons that often go beyond indicators of savings and investment. Manufacturing revamps old ways of earning a living and introduces important cultural changes, which when sustained, require a continuous rise in the autonomous component of investment (see figures 26 and 27).

Figure 24. Savings and foreign trade share

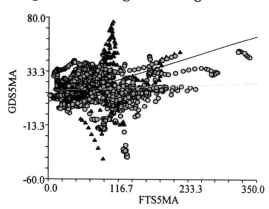

Figure 25. Investment and foreign trade share

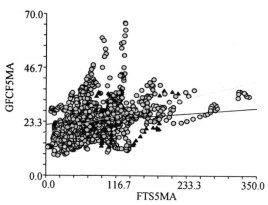

The oil economies lack a favourable resource mobilization potential in the manufacturing sector. Saudi Arabia's manufacturing share of GDP is constantly smaller than 10 per cent, putting it below the twenty-fifth percentile rank in the sample. The same holds for Kuwait and the United Arab Emirates.

Manufacturing plays a more important role in Egypt, Jordan and the Syrian Arab Republic. However, it is not associated with a great foreign trade share of GDP. This may signal the global comparative weakness of the manufacturing sector. The scatter plots in figures 28 and 29 underline the favourable impact of a high GDP share of manufactured goods, for example, fuel exports that have been controlled for.

These graphical presentations illustrate that the manufacturing base is in need of modernization and further expansion in terms of investment within an intraregional framework, based on the fact that a higher manufacturing share of exports corresponds to higher savings and investment rates.

Figure 26. Savings and manufacturing

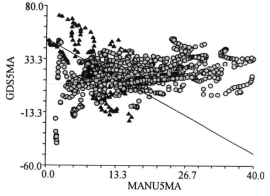

Figure 27. Investment and manufacturing

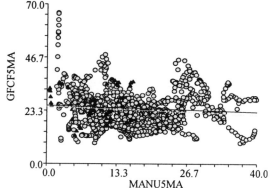

Figure 28. Savings and GDP share of manufactured goods without fuel exports

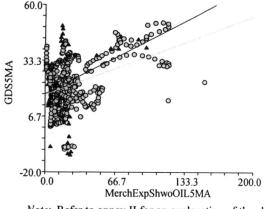

Figure 29. Investment and GDP share of manufactured goods without fuel exports

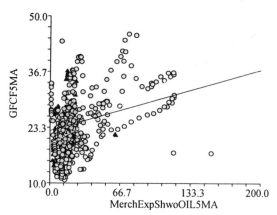

Note: Refer to annex II for an explanation of the abbreviations used.

14

3. *Capital market development*

In order to support the modernization and diversification of an economy, entrepreneurs need to be able to count on functioning capital markets. Data regarding market capitalization is scarce. Using available data on market capitalization, however, shows a considerable positive relationship with investment and a negative one with savings. Considerable capital outflows, risk-driven capital flight and lack of absorptive capacity in the oil economies generate an anomalous result for the ESCWA region (see figures 30 and 31).

Available data indicates that Kuwait, Saudi Arabia and Oman had market capitalization rates above the fiftieth percentile rank. Using interest rate spread as a proxy for capital market integration shows that investors in Bahrain, Kuwait and Oman enjoy among the lowest interest rate spreads in the developing world, with percentiles ranks between 5 and 15. Bahrain, however, is an exception, with an interest rate spread above the sixtieth percentile rank. Still, given the current extent of the complementary production structure in the ESCWA region, this leaves much room for symmetric integration in the real and financial economic spheres.

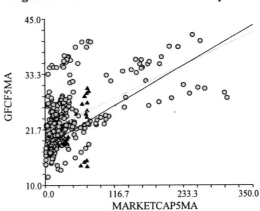

Figure 30. Savings and market capitalization   **Figure 31. Investment and market capitalization**

Note: Refer to annex II for an explanation of the abbreviations used.

4. *Educational attainment*

Figures 32 and 33 show that in the whole sample of developing countries educational attainment, as measured by secondary school enrolment data, is positively corrected with the gross fixed capital formation and savings.

The ESCWA region diverges with regard to educational attainment from the rest of the world in the sense that higher secondary educational attainment is correlated with lower fixed capital formation rates. The human capital aspect also extends to gender issues and the empowerment of women in the labour force. However, in the ESCWA region there is still a stark lack of complementarity between physical and human capital. Unless the quality of educational attainment is improved, problems are likely to persist. Using secondary enrolment as the measurement yardstick in 1999, Bahrain had the highest enrolment level, amounting to 88 per cent; followed by Qatar, with 78 per cent; the United Arab Emirates, with 67 per cent; Oman, 58 per cent; Kuwait, 49 per cent; Saudi Arabia, 42 per cent;[6] and Iraq with 33 per cent. National sources reports higher percentages of school enrolment. Only Bahrain, Oman, Qatar and the United Arab Emirates ranked above the fiftieth percentile rank, whereas the other oil economies for which data are available rank lower. The enrolment data for Kuwait is particularly erratic, which may be a consequence of the first Gulf war.

Secondary educational attainment among MDEs differs again substantially. Real progress took place in Egypt and Jordan. In this regard, Jordan increased secondary school enrolment from 53 to 76 per cent between 1980 and 1999, with most of the improvement taking place during the 1990s. This corresponds to an increase of the percentile rank from 53 to 87. Less data are available for Egypt. During the 1990s, however, Egypt increased secondary school enrolment from 65 in 1993 to 79 per cent in 1999. In terms of percentile

---

[6] National Sources report higher percentages of school enrolment.

rank, this was an improvement from 72 to 89. The Syrian Arab Republic, however, experienced a decline of secondary school enrolment during the 1990s. In 1990, secondary enrolment in that country was 45 per cent, dropping to 38 per cent in 1998, placing Syrian Arab Republic below the thirtieth percentile rank.

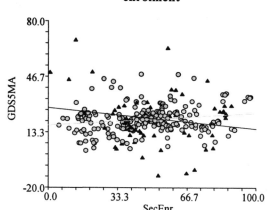

Figure 32. Savings and secondary school enrolment

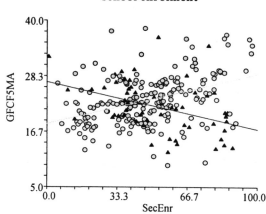

Figure 33. Investment and secondary school enrolment

5. *Equality of economic opportunities*

An important aspect of economic development is equality of economic opportunities. Economies with unequal opportunities are more likely to experience redistributive social conflict, governmental favouritism and leakages. Using a measurement of income inequality as a proxy for inequality of economic opportunities shows that countries with great income inequality exhibit lower levels of gross fixed capital formation (see figures 34 and 35).

The oil-exporting subregion's income inequality indicators are among the greatest in the world. Using the estimated household income inequality 2 indicator (EHII2) from the University of Texas Inequality Project, which reads the same as the Gini Coefficient, Kuwait, Oman and Qatar rank above the ninetieth percentile. Iraq, which has witnessed increasing inequalities since the 1980s, ranked above the eightieth percentile rank at the end of the 1990s. The United Arab Emirates, with the lowest indicator in the oil subregion, still ranks above the sixtieth percentile.

Inequality is also a problem among MDEs. By the end of the 1990s and in terms of percentile ranks, Egypt was above the fiftieth, the Syrian Arab Republic above the sixtieth and Jordan was above the ninetieth percentile. Yemen's inequality indicator was below the thirty-fifth percentile.

This indeed provides strong support for the idea that unequal economic opportunities in the ESCWA region forfeit the potential for higher investment, income and growth.

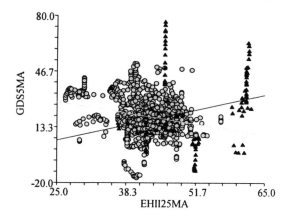

Figure 34. Savings and income inequality

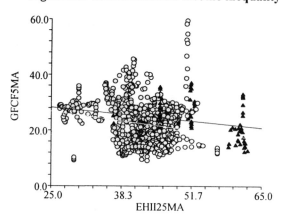

Figure 35. Investment and income inequality

Note: Refer to annex II for an explanation of the abbreviations used.

16

6. *Summary of supply side characteristics*

The analysis of the supply side in the ESCWA region shows that intraregional trade barriers represent severe impediments to growth in both oil economies and in MDEs. The manufacturing base is very small for the ESCWA region as a whole and this substantially reduces the global competitiveness of ESCWA region economies and the potential gains from trade. Educational attainment levels may be high in numbers but low in quality and tend not to fully complement the existing physical capital requirement. Finally, great inequalities reduce domestic saving by encouraging capital flight and thus represent a major obstacle to the capital formation of the region. Consequently, principal aspects of social development must also be addressed.

III. EMPIRICAL INVESTIGATION OF THE DETERMINANTS OF INVESTMENT CLIMATES

A. METHODOLOGY

This empirical section tests the demand and supply characteristics that are identified as being favourable to either savings or investment by using a multinominal logistic regression. The dependent variable is investment climate, which is defined either as super investor (SI), resource exporter (RX), resource importer (RM) or vicious cyclist (VC). The independent variables are the dummy fuel exporter, GDP, GDP per capita, standard deviation of per capita growth measured over five years, International Country Risk Guide index, government share of GDP, foreign trade share, manufacturing share of GDP and income inequality.

B. EMPIRICAL RESULTS

The empirical results, as summarized in the table below, signify that large and integrated regional markets support an enhanced investment climate. Similarly, high purchasing power is more likely to be found among resource exporters and super investors, and less likely to be located among resource importers and vicious cyclists. Growth volatility in the ESCWA region has reduced the likelihood of it becoming a super investor and resource importer and increased the likelihood of it becoming a resource exporter. Moreover, high growth volatility has also lowered the likelihood of it falling into the vicious cycle cluster, suggesting that the vicious cycle cluster is inhabited mainly by stagnating economies, which are rare in the ESCWA region. High country risk is statistically significant and tends to carry more weight with MDEs given their proximity to the conflict zones.

Overall, there is considerable support for the conclusion that small markets, low purchasing power, and high risk are statistically significant and that they tend to thwart development in the ESCWA region.

With regard to the oil economies, the dummy fuel exporter is a statistically significant counterweight to the diversified economies. In other words, supposing oil economies did not have oil, it is likely that they would display a production structure similar to that of MDEs. In view of different intraregional specialization potentials, this may lend support to the argument that the region can enjoy a complementary production structure, thereby opening the door to greater symmetric integration.

From the supply side, the regional foreign trade share is very significant, which can largely be attributed to oil. However, high foreign trade shares make it less likely that a country will become a vicious cyclist. If the manufacturing share is high, which is not the case in the ESCWA region, a country is more likely to be a super investor or resource exporter and less likely to be a vicious cyclist. Finally, countries with great inequalities in terms of economic opportunities are less likely to be found among resource importers and super investors, confirming the previous result that acute income inequality in the ESCWA region is counterproductive to gross fixed capital accumulation.

The regression is run against the variable 'average performer in saving and investment', which is a tolerance area for observations that are likely to change their climate characteristics often simply owing to their close location to the intersection between the 45-degree line and trend line of figure 7.

TABLE. MULTINOMINAL LOGISTIC REGRESSION RESULTS

		Dependent variable		$LN\left(\dfrac{P(Climate)}{P(Average)}\right)$		
			Coefficient	Z-value	Wald probability level
Fixed factors	Intercept	RM	12.6	4.2	0.00*
		RX	0.8	0.2	0.82
		SI	6.6	1.8	0.06**
		VC	10.2	4.1	0.00*
	Fuel exporter dummy	RM	-10.6	-0.2	0.88
		RX	1.5	2.1	0.04*
		SI	2.0	3.0	0.00*
		VC	-3.2	-5.4	0.00*

			Dependent variable	$LN\left(\dfrac{P(Climate)}{P(Average)}\right)$	
			Coefficient	Z-value	Wald probability level
Demand	GDP	RM	-0.00	-2.0	0.05*
		RX	0.00	-0.3	0.79
		SI	0.00	2.1	0.04*
		VC	-0.00	-5.6	0.00*
	GDP per capita	RM	-0.00	-2.0	0.05*
		RX	0.00	-0.3	0.79*
		SI	0.00	2.0	0.04*
		VC	-0.00	-5.6	0.00*
	Standard development of GDP per capita growth over 5 years	RM	-0.38	-3.5	0.00*
		RX	0.36	2.8	0.00*
		SI	-0.30	-2.6	0.00*
		VC	-0.12	-1.9	0.05**
	International Country Risk Guide index	RM	-0.09	-3.3	0.00*
		RX	0.00	0.0	0.96
		SI	-0.01	-0.2	0.85
		VC	-0.01	-0.8	0.42
	Government share of GDP	RM	0.05	1.3	0.19
		RX	-0.18	-2.6	0.01*
		SI	-0.04	-0.7	0.48
		VC	0.09	2.7	0.01*
Supply	Foreign trade share	RM	0.06	5.2	0.00*
		RX	0.03	2.6	0.01*
		SI	0.04	4.1	0.00*
		VC	-0.03	-4.5	0.00*
	Manufacturing share of GDP	RM	-0.07	-1.4	0.17
		RX	-0.17	-2.3	0.02*
		SI	0.09	1.6	0.10**
		VC	-0.06	-1.8	0.07**
	Income inequality	RM	-0.23	-4.1	0.00*
		RX	-0.05	-0.6	0.01
		SI	-0.26	-4.8	0.00*
		VC	-0.13	-3.2	0.00*

Source: Compiled by ESCWA.

Notes: The demarcation between supply and demand side parameters conceals many sides of the variable interplay that make one variable both a demand and a supply side component.

RM = Resource importer; RX = Resource exporter; SI = Super investor; VC = Vicious cyclist.

* denotes significant at the 5 per cent level.

** denotes significant at the 10 per cent level.

IV. POLICY RECOMMENDATIONS

Resource mobilization policies in the ESCWA region are needed on both the demand and supply sides. The ESCWA region requires a big push investment strategy to reverse declining investment rates. Unlike other developing regions, ESCWA is a region rich in capital. In the event that tensions recede, member countries could straightforwardly pursue a strategy of balanced growth without major drawbacks.

For the ESCWA region, the role of the state is not to invest in projects with balanced external economies, but rather to invest in projects that will unbalance the economy. Investment projects that are appropriate for unbalanced growth strategies must be integrated within the industrial culture. Unbalancing the economy must be part of a greater development and industrialization strategy, in which the State, in partnership with the private sector, attempts to identify those investment opportunities that free most entrepreneurial capacities in a broader intraregional market. In this instance the ESCWA region will benefit from integrating regional markets and shifting towards building the capacities of the manufacturing sector.

Adequate economic policy means providing incentives for the mobilization of productive resources from the demand and supply sides simultaneously. With regard to the demand side, an outstanding problem is risk. The ESCWA region must therefore provide extraterritorial investment guarantees for capital and labour. The ESCWA region must furthermore work towards establishing and funding automatic domestic stabilizers, for example, social security benefits, and in particular, unemployment insurance where feasible.

The ESCWA region faces another issue on the supply side, namely, the lost welfare potential from a regional division of labour. A strategy of development that encompasses the improvement of regional infrastructure and the expansion of the manufacturing sector, with the ultimate aim of ensuring higher capacity and productivity through new technologies and the training and development of human resources must be devised to tackle the dominance of the oil industry in the oil economies, similar export profiles among MDEs, and poor transportation and communication infrastructures.

The region primarily requires public investment in physical and institutional infrastructure to create greater external spillover effects. From an institutional perspective, this implies, for example, the creation of new regulations that reduce intraregional trade barriers and improve the quality of infrastructure.

Small, regional fragmented markets set back potential entrepreneurial capital. This is exacerbated by high-income inequalities, poorly developed capital markets and low levels of educational attainment.

A necessary unbalancing effect on the economy, however, must first stem from bigger markets and more intraregional competition. This is only possible with a credible commitment to regional market integration and harmonized policies and procedures that facilitate trade within the region.

However, even if markets in the ESCWA region are unbalanced to awaken entrepreneurial capacities, it is unlikely that in an environment with the greatest inequalities of income and economic opportunities, limited capital and real markets will be able to provide entrepreneurs with ample investment opportunities or be able to stem the flow of capital out of the region. Therefore, public and private investment packages that encourage the potential for increased investment opportunities and that bridge income inequality gaps are recommended. With this in mind, and in order to finance such programmes, mild progressive taxation is no longer a choice; it is an imperative. That is particularly the case as the ESCWA region has the highest income inequality profile in the world.

COUNTRY LIST

1.	Afghanistan	45.	Libyan Arab Jamahiriya
2.	Algeria	46.	Malaysia
3.	American Samoa	47.	Maldives
4.	Antigua and Barbuda	48.	Malta
5.	Argentina	49.	Marshall Islands
6.	Bahrain	50.	Mexico
7.	Bangladesh	51.	Micronesia (Federated States of)
8.	Barbados	52.	Mongolia
9.	Belize	53.	Morocco
10.	Bhutan	54.	Myanmar
11.	Bolivia	55.	Nepal
12.	Brazil	56.	Nicaragua
13.	Cambodia	57.	Oman
14.	Chile	58.	Pakistan
15.	China	59.	Palau
16.	Colombia	60.	Panama
17.	Costa Rica	61.	Papua New Guinea
18.	Cuba	62.	Paraguay
19.	Djibouti	63.	Peru
20.	Dominica	64.	Philippines
21.	Dominican Republic	65.	Puerto Rico
22.	Ecuador	66.	Qatar
23.	Egypt	67.	Samoa
24.	El Salvador	68.	Saudi Arabia
25.	Fiji	69.	Singapore
26.	Grenada	70.	Solomon Islands
27.	Guatemala	71.	Sri Lanka
28.	Guyana	72.	St. Kitts and Nevis
29.	Haiti	73.	St. Lucia
30.	Honduras	74.	St. Vincent and the Grenadines
31.	Hong Kong, China	75.	Suriname
32.	India	76.	Syrian Arab Republic
33.	Indonesia	77.	Thailand
34.	Iran (Islamic Republic of)	78.	Tonga
35.	Iraq	79.	Trinidad and Tobago
36.	Israel	80.	Tunisia
37.	Jamaica	81.	Turkey
38.	Jordan	82.	United Arab Emirates
39.	Kiribati	83.	Uruguay
40.	Korea (Democratic People's Republic of)	84.	Vanuatu
41.	Korea (Republic of)	85.	Venezuela
42.	Kuwait	86.	Viet Nam
43.	Lao People's Democratic Republic	87.	West Bank and Gaza Strip
44.	Lebanon	88.	Yemen

VARIABLE LIST AND TECHNICAL DETAILS[6]

(a)   *Technical details*

All variables used in the empirical analysis are computed as five-year moving averages according to the following, and then abbreviated as '5MA':

$$\text{Observation in } t = \frac{\sum_{t-2}^{t+2} \text{Observation}_t}{5}$$

(b)   *Investment climate indicators*

GDS
Gross domestic saving, as a percentage of gross domestic product (GDP)

GFCF
Gross fixed capital formation, as a percentage of GDP

CLIMATE
The trend line was estimated with pooled regression. The area 'average' was computed according to the distance between the observation and the intersection of the 45-degree and trend line. If the distance fell below the twentieth percentile rank (distance<5.956) the climate 'average' was assigned.

Countries are assigned one of five different investment climates (INVCLIMATE) according to the graph on the right:

SI: Super investor;
RX: Resource exporter;
RM: Resource importer;
VC: Vicious cyclists;
AVG: Average.

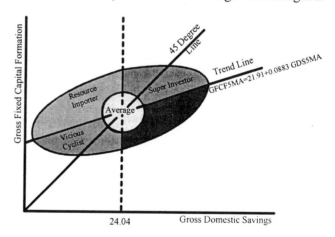

(c)   *Demand side indicators*

GDP
GDP in 1995 US dollars

GDPCAP
GDP per capita in 1995 US dollars

GDPCAPgr
Real GDP per capita growth

GDPCAPVOL
The standard deviation of GDPCAPgr over five years

---

[6]   World Bank Group, World Development Indicators database.

ICRG
International Country Risk Guide index

DEBT
Central government debt, as a total percentage of GDP

GOV
Central government expenditure, as a total percentage of GDP

(d)   *Supply side indicators*

FTS
Foreign trade share, as a total percentage of GDP

FTSyc
Residual of regressing GDPCAP on FTS

MerchX
Merchandise export, as a total percentage of GDP

MerchXwO
Merchandise exports of goods excluding oil exports, as a total percentage of GDP. This is based on ESCWA calculations using the following variables: (1) fuel exports, as a percentage of merchandise exports (see World Development Indicators (WDI) database); (2) Merchandise exports, in current dollars (see WDI database); and (3) United States Bureau of Labour Statistics data to convert current dollars into 1995 dollars.

Subsequently, MerchXwO = [(2)-(3)-[(1) -(2) -(3)/100]/GDP

MANU
Manufacturing, value added, as a percentage of GDP

MARKETCAP
Market capitalization of listed companies, as a percentage of GDP

SPREAD
Interest rate spread, lending minus deposit rate

SECENR
School enrolment, secondary, percentage net

EHII2[7]
Estimated household income inequality two indicator

---

[7]   University of Texas Inequality Project. Available at: http://utip.gov.utexas.edu/data.htm.

COUNTRY TABLES AND GRAPHS

BAHRAIN

Gross domestic savings, gross fixed capital formation and GDP per capita growth over time

Year	Investment climate indicators		
	GDS5MA	GFCF5MA	INVCLIMATE
1982	49.8 (98.5)	35.61 (93.7)	SI (93.6)
1983	48.32 (97.9)	36.2 (94.5)	SI (91.3)
1984	45.88 (97.1)	36.81 (95.1)	SI (87.7)
1985	44.27 (96.4)	34.72 (92)	SI (80.9)
1986	42.36 (95.7)	30.39 (85.5)	SI (66.8)
1987	40.44 (94.8)	25.54 (65.1)	SI (56.3)
1988	38.41 (93.3)	22.57 (48.8)	RX (64.3)
1989	33.89 (88.8)	20.08 (34.5)	RX (51.7)
1990	29.22 (82.4)	19.9 (33.4)	RX (8)
1991	25.9 (77.3)	20.68 (37.7)	AVG (NA)
1992	24.14 (72.7)	20.7 (37.8)	AVG (NA)
1993	21.89 (65.7)	20.38 (36.5)	AVG (NA)
1994	23.52 (70.8)	18.9 (28)	AVG (NA)
1995	25.51 (76.6)	16.97 (17.1)	RX (14.9)
1996	25.65 (77)	15.13 (10.1)	RX (40.2)
1997	25.72 (77.2)	13.86 (6.4)	RX (50.5)
1998	27.6 (80)	13.1 (4.6)	RX (58.6)
1999	29.19 (82.2)	13.29 (5.2)	RX (60.9)

Source: World Bank Group, World Development Indicators (WDI) database.

Note: Yellow circles indicate gross domestic savings; red triangles, gross fixed capital formation; and green quadrants, GDP per capita growth (all observations are five-year moving averages).
Variables and other technical details are explained in annex II;
All indicators are assigned their percentile ranks in the sample. Percentile ranks are in parentheses next to the absolute value and are denoted in column headings as 'PC';
A hyphen (-) indicates that the item is not applicable.

BAHRAIN

Demand side indicators

Year	GDP(PC)	GDPCAP(PC)	GDPCAPgr(PC)	GDPCAPVOL(PC)	ICRG(PC)	DEBT(PC)	GOV(PC)
1990	4 389.8 (36.6)	8 795.2 (91)	3.36 (69.1)	4.74 (71.9)	63.1 (51.5)	16.7 (14.8)	24.08 (87.1)
1991	4 714.4 (37.7)	9 197.2 (91.5)	4.45 (82)	5.4 (78.5)	66.8 (63.2)	16.92 (15.3)	23.66 (86.3)
1992	5 033.4 (39)	9 568.6 (91.8)	4.27 (80.8)	5.72 (80.8)	70.3 (75.9)	16.73 (15)	22.95 (84.6)
1993	5 360.8 (40.9)	9 921.2 (92.2)	4.03 (77.9)	5.88 (81.9)	73.7 (87.4)	18.38 (18.6)	22.28 (82.6)
1994	5 641.6 (42.4)	10 109.8 (92.3)	2.06 (51.7)	4.89 (73.4)	75.7 (92.1)	18.27 (18)	21.65 (81.5)
1995	5 897.4 (42.8)	10 208.6 (92.6)	1.1 (37.5)	4.79 (72.2)	75.65 (92)	17.4 (15.8)	20.77 (79.5)
1996	6 084.8 (43.5)	10 153.6 (92.4)	-0.51 (21)	1.92 (26.5)	74.6 (90.1)	17.76 (16.8)	20.47 (78.2)
1997	6 327 (44.4)	10 251.2 (92.8)	0.96 (35.7)	1.53 (17.1)	72.86 (84.9)	18.92 (18.9)	20.43 (77.6)
1998	6 598.6 (45.1)	10 446.8 (93)	1.88 (49.4)	2.26 (34.4)	72.02 (81.9)	21.38 (22.3)	19.77 (75.4)
1999	6 822 (45.7)	10 627.4 (93.2)	1.74 (47)	2.4 (37.4)	73.32 (86.7)	24.35 (26.4)	19.42 (74)

Supply side indicators

Year	FTS(PC)	FTSyc(PC)	MerchX (PC)	MerchXwO (PC)	MANU (PC)	MARKETCAP (PC)	SPREAD (PC)	SecEnr (PC)	EHII2 (PC)
1990	186.2 (96.7)	74.46 (94.3)	85.54 (94.6)	19.14 (62.9)	16.38 (60.6)	-	-	84.91 (94.8)	-
1991	184.56 (96.5)	71.94 (93.3)	83.93 (94.4)	20.11 (66)	15.82 (57.4)	-	-	84.472 (94.5)	-
1992	178.34 (95.8)	64.94 (91.6)	79.9 (94.1)	21.87 (73.2)	15.59 (56.4)	-	-	85.682 (96.1)	-
1993	166.8 (94)	52.68 (88.3)	73.07 (92.9)	24.06 (79.3)	16.05 (58.8)	-	-	85.4 (95.9)	-
1994	163.5 (93.4)	49.01 (87.1)	71.24 (92.7)	25.48 (80.9)	-	-	7.28 (66.6)	85.241 (95.6)	-
1995	156.99 (92.6)	42.31 (84.6)	69.4 (92.1)	-	-	-	7.04 (65)	84.318 (94.2)	-
1996	149.77 (92.1)	35.19 (81.8)	64.78 (91)	-	-	-	6.9 (63.4)	82.737 (93.1)	-
1997	146.6 (91.4)	31.83 (79.6)	62.56 (89.8)	-	-	-	6.94 (64)	84.179 (93.7)	-
1998	145.23 (91.1)	30.09 (78.7)	62.59 (89.9)	-	-	-	6.9 (63.4)	80.152 (91.2)	-
1999	140.38 (90.1)	24.9 (74.6)	60.85 (89.4)	-	-	-	7.06 (65.2)	88.251 (97.2)	-

EGYPT

Gross domestic savings, gross fixed capital formation and GDP per capita growth over time

	Investment climate indicators		
Year	GDS5MA	GFCF5MA	INVCLIMATE
1975	12.22 (24.5)	19.36 (30.6)	VC (53)
1976	13.9 (29.8)	22.42 (47.1)	VC (38)
1977	15.6 (37.7)	25.18 (63.5)	RM (19.4)
1978	16.18 (40.5)	25.19 (63.5)	RM (16.4)
1979	15.66 (38)	26.25 (68.2)	RM (22)
1980	15.01 (34.5)	27.68 (76.2)	RM (32.2)
1981	15.29 (36.3)	28.11 (78)	RM (31.9)
1982	15.24 (36.2)	27.54 (75.8)	RM (29.5)
1983	15.12 (35.3)	27.65 (76.1)	RM (31.3)
1984	15.07 (34.9)	26.7 (71)	RM (28.3)
1985	15.21 (35.8)	26.25 (68.2)	RM (25.9)
1986	15.07 (34.9)	27.23 (73.6)	RM (30.7)
1987	15.73 (38.5)	27.99 (77.5)	RM (26.8)
1988	16.05 (40)	28.34 (79.5)	RM (25.6)
1989	15.92 (39.5)	28.31 (79)	RM (26.5)
1990	15.82 (38.8)	26.66 (70.8)	RM (21.7)
1991	15.05 (34.9)	23.01 (52.2)	VC (27.3)
1992	13.86 (29.5)	20.21 (35.4)	VC (41.5)
1993	13.06 (27.4)	18.06 (22.8)	VC (52.3)
1994	12.59 (25.7)	16.82 (16.5)	VC (57.7)
1995	11.89 (23.1)	16.72 (15.9)	VC (63.5)
1996	11.51 (21.9)	17.66 (20.4)	VC (61.9)
1997	11.66 (22.4)	18.28 (24.1)	VC (58.4)
1998	11.56 (22.1)	18.58 (26)	VC (58.1)
1999	11.47 (21.8)	18.38 (24.7)	VC (59.8)

Source: World Bank Group, World Development Indicators (WDI) database.

Note: Yellow circles indicate gross domestic savings; red triangles, gross fixed capital formation; and green quadrants, GDP per capita growth (all observations are five-year moving averages). Variables and other technical details are explained in annex II; All indicators are assigned their percentile ranks in the sample. Percentile ranks are in parentheses next to the absolute value and are denoted in column headings as 'PC'; A hyphen (-) indicates that the item is not applicable.

EGYPT

Demand side indicators

Year	GDP(PC)	GDPCAP(PC)	GDPCAPgr(PC)	GDPCAPVOL(PC)	ICRG(PC)	DEBT(PC)	GOV(PC)
1990	50 036.2 (75.6)	953.6 (28)	1.95 (50)	1.77 (22.5)	52.4 (20.3)	-	11.89 (37)
1991	51 917.8 (76.1)	968.2 (28.2)	1.54 (43.7)	1.76 (22.1)	57.7 (33.8)	-	11.14 (32.6)
1992	53 779.6 (76.6)	981.6 (28.6)	1.41 (41.6)	1.69 (20.6)	62.8 (50.6)	-	10.67 (28.9)
1993	55 628.4 (77.1)	994.2 (29)	1.28 (39.8)	1.52 (17)	67.5 (66.1)	-	10.52 (27.2)
1994	57 970.2 (77.8)	1 015.4 (29.4)	2.12 (52.3)	0.88 (5.2)	69.2 (71.1)	-	10.36 (25.5)
1995	60 549.6 (79.2)	1 039.8 (30.2)	2.37 (56.3)	1.08 (8.3)	70.05 (74.8)	-	10.3 (24.7)
1996	63 425.4 (80.1)	1 068.2 (31.4)	2.73 (60.7)	0.6 (1.9)	70.2 (75.5)	-	10.3 (24.7)
1997	66 740.4 (81.2)	1 102.8 (32)	3.21 (67.1)	0.7 (2.9)	69.46 (72.8)	-	10.28 (24.4)
1998	70 275.8 (82.3)	1 139.4 (32.6)	3.31 (68.5)	0.63 (2.4)	69.12 (70.7)	-	10.12 (22.6)
1999	73 659.8 (82.8)	1 172 (33.3)	2.89 (63)	1.22 (10.8)	69.38 (72.1)	-	10.43 (26.4)

Supply side indicators

Year	FTS(PC)	FTSyc(PC)	MerchX (PC)	MerchXwO (PC)	MANU (PC)	MARKETCAP (PC)	SPREAD (PC)	SecEnr (PC)	EHII2 (PC)
1990	55.99 (38.4)	-11.83 (48.4)	10.32 (20.8)	6.57 (14.6)	17.35 (66.9)	5.68 (9.6)	-	-	42.12 (34.5)
1991	57.17 (39.5)	-10.95 (49)	8.29 (14.1)	5.01 (6.4)	17.14 (65.6)	6.29 (10.6)	-	-	42.74 (40.4)
1992	57.34 (39.7)	-11.05 (48.9)	6.88 (7.7)	3.92 (4.3)	16.96 (64.2)	7.07 (11.5)	-	-	43.29 (45.8)
1993	56.78 (39.2)	-11.86 (48.2)	6.43 (6.1)	3.51 (3.4)	16.9 (63.9)	8.94 (15.1)	-	65.2 (72.2)	43.7 (50.2)
1994	53.28 (35.6)	-15.78 (41.9)	5.9 (3.5)	3.34 (3.1)	17.13 (65.5)	11.69 (23.6)	5.98 (53.8)	-	44.1 (52.4)
1995	50.16 (32.4)	-19.37 (34.5)	5.78 (3.4)	3.28 (3)	17.42 (67.1)	15.63 (34.5)	5.11 (42.3)	-	44.29 (54.4)
1996	47.14 (28.5)	-22.92 (29)	5.43 (2.7)	3.27 (2.8)	17.84 (69.3)	19.95 (43.3)	4.58 (32.2)	67.455 (75.4)	44.77 (57)
1997	44.74 (25.4)	-25.95 (25.6)	5.06 (1.9)	3.07 (2.7)	18.31 (71.6)	25.68 (50)	4.39 (29.5)	-	44.91 (57.9)
1998	42.58 (23)	-28.75 (23)	4.99 (1.8)	-	18.69 (73.6)	28.77 (55.4)	4.03 (25.7)	-	44.97 (58.2)
1999	41.41 (21.9)	-30.48 (21.5)	4.79 (1.7)	-	19 (75.3)	29.49 (56.6)	3.79 (22.6)	79.034 (89.1)	45.01 (58.6)

IRAQ

Demand side indicators

Year	GDP(PC)	GDPCAP(PC)	GDPCAPgr(PC)	GDPCAPVOL(PC)	ICRG(PC)	DEBT(PC)	GOV(PC)
1990	-	-	-	-	29.6 (0.9)	-	-
1991	-	-	-	-	28.4 (0.6)	-	-
1992	-	-	-	-	26.6 (0)	-	-
1993	-	-	-	-	27.8 (0.5)	-	-
1994	-	-	-	-	30.2 (1.2)	-	-
1995	-	-	-	-	32.25 (1.5)	-	-
1996	-	-	-	-	35.2 (2.7)	-	-
1997	-	-	-	-	37.96 (3.6)	-	-
1998	-	-	-	-	41.06 (6.3)	-	-
1999	-	-	-	-	43.52 (8.4)	-	-

Supply side indicators

Year	FTS(PC)	FTSyc(PC)	MerchX (PC)	MerchXwO (PC)	MANU (PC)	MARKETCAP (PC)	SPREAD (PC)	SecEnr (PC)	EHII2 (PC)
1990	-	-	-	-	-	-	-	-	44.34 (54.9)
1991	-	-	-	-	-	-	-	-	44.94 (58)
1992	-	-	-	-	-	-	-	37.275 (28.3)	46.07 (69)
1993	-	-	-	-	-	-	-	-	46.89 (74.7)
1994	-	-	-	-	-	-	-	-	47.53 (80)
1995	-	-	-	-	-	-	-	-	48.08 (85.5)
1996	-	-	-	-	-	-	-	-	48.54 (86.5)
1997	-	-	-	-	-	-	-	-	48.57 (86.7)
1998	-	-	-	-	-	-	-	-	48.57 (86.7)
1999	-	-	-	-	-	-	-	32.989 (22)	48.57 (86.7)

Source: World Bank Group, WDI database.

Note: All indicators are assigned their percentile ranks in the sample. Percentile ranks are in parentheses next to the absolute value and are denoted in column headings as "PC". A hyphen (-) indicates that the item is not applicable.

JORDAN

Gross domestic savings, gross fixed capital formation and GDP per capita growth over time

	Investment climate indicators		
Year	GDS5MA	GFCF5MA	INVCLIMATE
1978	-13.04 (1.6)	34.99 (92.7)	RM (92.5)
1979	-12.04 (1.8)	37.08 (95.3)	RM (91.9)
1980	-12.85 (1.7)	36.45 (94.8)	RM (92.8)
1981	-12.58 (1.7)	35.52 (93.3)	RM (92.2)
1982	-10.52 (2.3)	34.27 (91.5)	RM (90.4)
1983	-12.02 (1.8)	31 (86.6)	RM (91.3)
1984	-11.39 (2.1)	26.14 (67.8)	RM (89.2)
1985	-9.07 (2.6)	22.83 (50.9)	RM (87.4)
1986	-6.32 (3.3)	21.51 (42.2)	RM (84.1)
1987	-3.29 (3.7)	20.86 (38.5)	VC (98.6)
1988	-0.05 (4.4)	22.25 (46.3)	RM (80)
1989	1.58 (5.4)	23.22 (53.3)	RM (77.6)
1990	2.31 (6.2)	24.91 (62)	RM (77)
1991	3.2 (7)	27.02 (72.6)	RM (76.4)
1992	4.19 (8.1)	28.67 (80.8)	RM (74.9)
1993	6.32 (10.7)	29.31 (82.8)	RM (71.3)
1994	6.83 (11.4)	30.36 (85.5)	RM (70.7)
1995	7.22 (12.1)	29.71 (84.1)	RM (69.5)
1996	6.5 (10.9)	27.29 (73.9)	RM (69.8)
1997	5.97 (10)	25.66 (65.7)	RM (70.4)
1998	3.72 (7.6)	24.93 (62.3)	RM (74.6)
1999	2.91 (6.7)	24.31 (59.1)	RM (76.7)

Source: World Bank Group, World Development Indicators (WDI) database.

Note: Yellow circles indicate gross domestic savings; red triangles, gross fixed capital formation; and green quadrants, GDP per capita growth (all observations are five-year moving averages).

Variables and other technical details are explained in annex II;
All indicators are assigned their percentile ranks in the sample. Percentile ranks are in parentheses next to the absolute value and are denoted in column headings as 'PC';
A hyphen (-) indicates that the item is not applicable.

JORDAN

Demand side indicators

Year	GDP(PC)	GDPCAP(PC)	GDPCAPgr(PC)	GDPCAPVOL(PC)	ICRG(PC)	DEBT(PC)	GOV(PC)
1990	5167.4 (39.8)	1579.4 (45.3)	-4.11 (5.2)	10.82 (95.5)	51.7 (18.9)	129.04 (95.3)	25.06 (89)
1991	5284.6 (40.4)	1517.8 (43.4)	-3.06 (8)	10.93 (95.7)	55.5 (27.5)	133.88 (95.9)	24.1 (87.2)
1992	5611 (42.2)	1521 (43.4)	0.44 (29.1)	7.94 (91.4)	60.7 (43.3)	131.71 (95.5)	23.36 (85.6)
1993	6009.8 (43.2)	1541.8 (44.5)	1.57 (44.4)	7.79 (90.8)	66.8 (63.2)	125.81 (94.8)	23.04 (84.8)
1994	6419.6 (44.5)	1586.6 (45.7)	3.16 (66.6)	5.61 (80)	71.5 (79.7)	119.82 (94.5)	22.67 (83.9)
1995	6687.4 (45.3)	1595.8 (45.8)	0.59 (30.8)	1.5 (16.2)	73.05 (85.6)	109.48 (93.5)	23.4 (85.7)
1996	6943.4 (46.1)	1604.4 (46.1)	0.56 (30.2)	1.52 (16.9)	74.55 (89.9)	104.74 (92.4)	23.87 (86.7)
1997	7184.2 (46.7)	1610 (46.4)	0.37 (28.2)	1.51 (16.6)	74.05 (88.4)	101.7 (92.3)	24.2 (87.5)
1998	7404.2 (47.4)	1609 (46.3)	-0.06 (24.2)	0.65 (2.5)	73.11 (86.2)	99.71 (91.9)	24.56 (88)
1999	7662 (47.8)	1615.2 (46.5)	0.38 (28.4)	0.62 (2.3)	72.71 (84.1)	97.14 (90.6)	24.32 (87.7)

Supply side indicators

Year	FTS(PC)	FTSyc(PC)	MerchX (PC)	MerchXwO (PC)	MANU (PC)	MARKETCAP (PC)	SPREAD (PC)	SecEnr (PC)	EHII2 (PC)
1990	134.77 (88.5)	56.98 (89.3)	25.35 (62)	-	12.96 (45.8)	52.33 (79.6)	-	-	51.61 (92.7)
1991	138.39 (89.7)	61.39 (90.7)	24.87 (60.9)	-	13.56 (48.1)	62.21 (81.5)	-	32.807 (21.7)	52.09 (93.6)
1992	135.35 (88.6)	58.3 (89.8)	23.74 (58)	-	14.29 (51.3)	66.33 (82.7)	2.81 (13)	32.249 (21.2)	52.24 (94)
1993	129.03 (86.6)	51.72 (87.8)	23.77 (58.1)	23.77 (78.9)	14.29 (51.3)	70.09 (84.8)	2.98 (14.1)	35.4 (25)	52.28 (94)
1994	126.43 (85.7)	48.55 (86.8)	23.67 (57.8)	-	14.25 (51.1)	71.06 (86.3)	3.08 (15)	-	52.23 (93.9)
1995	124.06 (84.4)	46.07 (86.1)	24 (58.9)	-	14.2 (51.1)	73.39 (87.2)	3.12 (15.4)	41.441 (35.9)	52.19 (93.8)
1996	119.71 (82.3)	41.61 (84.4)	24.25 (60)	-	14.62 (52.1)	70.8 (86)	3.33 (18.3)	-	51.57 (92.7)
1997	117.03 (81.1)	38.86 (83.4)	24.05 (59.1)	-	14.62 (52.1)	70.53 (85.7)	3.46 (19.6)	-	51.27 (92.1)
1998	114.51 (80)	36.35 (82.4)	23.13 (55.6)	-	14.77 (52.5)	68.52 (83.9)	3.83 (23.5)	79.403 (90.1)	51.09 (91.9)
1999	111.3 (78.4)	33.07 (80.5)	22.84 (54.4)	22.84 (76.9)	15.12 (54.5)	69.87 (84.5)	4.3 (28.3)	75.872 (87.1)	51.02 (91.8)

KUWAIT

Gross domestic savings, gross fixed capital formation and GDP per capita growth over time

Year	Investment climate indicators		
	GDS5MA	GFCF5MA	INVCLIMATE
1975	63.64 (99.5)	12.33 (2.8)	RX (98.8)
1976	61.96 (99.4)	14.24 (7.5)	RX (97.7)
1977	58.94 (99.2)	15.38 (10.9)	RX (95.4)
1978	57.1 (99.2)	15.5 (11.3)	RX (94.2)
1979	54.25 (98.9)	15.64 (12.1)	RX (90.8)
1980	49.33 (98.2)	16.24 (13.9)	RX (88.5)
1981	46.06 (97.3)	17.54 (20)	RX (80.4)
1982	40.8 (95)	19.46 (31.2)	RX (74.7)
1983	35.17 (90.6)	20.9 (38.9)	RX (59.7)
1984	29.69 (82.9)	22.17 (46.1)	AVG (NA)
1985	30.82 (84.4)	20.93 (39.1)	RX (24.1)
1986	27.97 (80.6)	18.65 (26.5)	RX (9.1)
1987	25.34 (76.1)	16.58 (15)	RX (26.4)
1988	20.28 (58.9)	16.22 (13.8)	VC (22.6)
1989	2.83 (6.5)	19.75 (32.7)	VC (92.3)
1990	-2.04 (3.9)	20.34 (36.2)	VC (98)
1991	-1.97 (4)	20.63 (37.5)	VC (97.9)
1992	-1.7 (4)	21.13 (39.9)	VC (97.7)
1993	2.55 (6.3)	20.3 (35.8)	VC (92.8)
1994	21.66 (64.7)	15.27 (10.5)	VC (27.7)
1995	25.4 (76.4)	14.03 (6.9)	RX (45.9)
1996	23.58 (70.9)	14.79 (9.1)	VC (29.4)
1997	23 (69)	15.13 (10.1)	VC (26.5)
1998	24.9 (75)	13.86 (6.4)	RX (48.2)
1999	24.37 (73.7)	12.75 (3.9)	RX (56.3)

Source: World Bank Group, World Development Indicators (WDI) database.

Note: Yellow circles indicate gross domestic savings; red triangles, gross fixed capital formation; and green quadrants, GDP per capita growth (all observations are five-year moving averages).

Variables and other technical details are explained in annex II; All indicators are assigned their percentile ranks in the sample. Percentile ranks are in parentheses next to the absolute value and are denoted in column headings as 'PC'; A hyphen (-) indicates that the item is not applicable.

31

KUWAIT

Demand side indicators

Year	GDP(PC)	GDPCAP(PC)	GDPCAPgr(PC)	GDPCAPVOL(PC)	ICRG(PC)	DEBT(PC)	GOV(PC)
1990	-	-	-	-	56.9 (32.1)	-	44.44 (99.1)
1991	-	-	-	-	59.1 (38.4)	-	46.36 (99.2)
1992	-	-	-	-	61.5 (45.6)	-	48.06 (99.5)
1993	-	-	-	-	72.2 (82.3)	-	46.9 (99.3)
1994	23 703.2 (63.6)	15 416.2 (96.5)	-	-	77.8 (94.5)	-	37.19 (98.3)
1995	25 446.4 (64.5)	15 855.2 (96.8)	4.21 (80.1)	15.61 (98.7)	79 (95.7)	-	31.49 (95.6)
1996	26 169.8 (64.8)	15 548.8 (96.6)	-1.87 (12.1)	5.5 (78.8)	79.05 (95.8)	-	30.62 (94.9)
1997	26 412.6 (64.9)	14 936.8 (96.3)	-3.87 (5.9)	3.72 (60.3)	77.91 (94.6)	-	29.38 (94.1)
1998	26 613.8 (65)	14 363.8 (96.1)	-3.61 (6.5)	4.04 (64)	78.17 (94.8)	-	27.31 (91.6)
1999	26 902 (65.2)	13 987.4 (95.9)	-2.57 (9.6)	2.72 (44.1)	78.87 (95.6)	-	27.04 (91.4)

Supply side indicators

Year	FTS(PC)	FTSyc(PC)	MerchX (PC)	MerchXwO (PC)	MANU (PC)	MARKETCAP (PC)	SPREAD (PC)	SecEnr (PC)	EHI2 (PC)
1990	104.92 (74.9)	-	-	-	10.63 (36.1)	-	-	-	61.1 (97)
1991	105.23 (75.2)	-	-	-	9.67 (30.8)	-	-	45.198 (41.6)	60.02 (96.4)
1992	105.11 (75.1)	-	-	-	8.98 (25.5)	-	-	-	59.5 (96.3)
1993	103.82 (74.2)	-	-	-	8.84 (24.8)	-	-	54.1 (55.3)	59.13 (96.2)
1994	93.84 (67.3)	-28.99 (22.8)	47.4 (83.9)	2.51 (2.3)	-	-	1.55 (5.8)	-	58.84 (96.2)
1995	93.69 (67.2)	-29.7 (22.1)	49.51 (85.2)	3.63 (3.9)	-	59.41 (80.9)	2.04 (8.8)	61.813 (68.9)	58.72 (96.1)
1996	94.89 (68.7)	-28.11 (23.9)	46.89 (83.6)	4.54 (5)	-	65.45 (82.4)	2.39 (11)	61.107 (67.5)	60.1 (96.5)
1997	93.88 (67.4)	-28.33 (23.7)	46.11 (82.7)	5.76 (10.3)	-	69.61 (84.2)	2.57 (11.6)	58.262 (63.2)	60.98 (97)
1998	92.8 (66.3)	-28.63 (23)	49.03 (84.9)	-	-	70.4 (85.4)	2.8 (12.9)	49.717 (49.3)	61.72 (98.4)
1999	92.69 (66)	-28.22 (23.8)	48.03 (84.2)	-	-	-	2.94 (13.8)	-	62.38 (98.9)

LEBANON

Gross domestic savings, gross fixed capital formation and GDP per capita growth over time

Year	Investment climate indicators		
	GDS5MA	GFCF5MA	INVCLIMATE
1992	-42.48 (0)	24.71 (60.7)	RM (97.9)
1993	-33.22 (0.6)	28.32 (79.3)	RM (97)
1994	-26.44 (0.7)	30.41 (85.6)	RM (96.4)
1995	-21.43 (0.7)	30.66 (86.2)	RM (95.8)
1996	-15.6 (1.2)	30.66 (86.2)	RM (93.7)
1997	-11.47 (2)	28.49 (80.3)	RM (89.8)
1998	-9.25 (2.5)	24.94 (62.4)	RM (88)
1999	-8.07 (2.9)	22.72 (50.1)	RM (85.3)

Source: World Bank Group, World Development Indicators (WDI) database.

Note: Yellow circles indicate gross domestic savings; red triangles, gross fixed capital formation; and green quadrants, GDP per capita growth (all observations are five-year moving **averages**).

Variables and other technical details are explained in annex II;
All indicators are assigned their percentile ranks in the sample. Percentile ranks are in parentheses next to the absolute value and are denoted in column headings as 'PC';
A hyphen (-) indicates that the item is not applicable.

LEBANON

Demand side indicators

Year	GDP(PC)	GDPCAP(PC)	GDPCAPgr(PC)	GDPCAPVOL(PC)	ICRG(PC)	DEBT(PC)	GOV(PC)
1990	7494 (47.6)	2 058.2 (56.5)	-	-	33.8 (2.3)	-	-
1991	7 709.2 (48.1)	2 067.2 (56.8)	4.66 (83.5)	30.28 (99.7)	41.1 (6.4)	-	18.15 (69.1)
1992	8 808.4 (50.1)	2 321.2 (61)	14.58 (99.8)	14.5 (98.4)	49.4 (15.9)	-	17.43 (65.2)
1993	9 781 (51.5)	2 532.2 (63.5)	10.67 (99.3)	13.93 (97.9)	55.8 (28.8)	-	14.48 (51)
1994	10 364.8 (52.3)	2 633 (65.1)	4 (77.4)	1.63 (19.6)	59.6 (39.3)	-	12.88 (43.3)
1995	10 963.2 (53.4)	2 735.4 (66.3)	3.97 (76.8)	1.68 (20.5)	62.4 (49.1)	80.06 (83.9)	12.1 (38.7)
1996	11 507.2 (54)	2 822.4 (67.5)	3.26 (67.9)	1.89 (25.3)	61.55 (45.9)	92.62 (88.5)	11.63 (35.5)
1997	11 921.4 (54.4)	2 876.8 (68.4)	1.98 (50.7)	1.78 (22.9)	59.41 (39.1)	105.77 (92.8)	11.6 (35.4)
1998	12 199.8 (54.9)	2 899.8 (68.9)	0.82 (33.9)	1.61 (19.2)	59.31 (38.7)	-	13.42 (46.4)
1999	12 421.6 (55.2)	2 910.6 (69)	0.39 (28.5)	1.45 (14.9)	58.17 (36)	-	14.85 (52.8)

Supply side indicators

Year	FTS(PC)	FTSyc(PC)	MerchX (PC)	MerchXwO (PC)	MANU (PC)	MARKETCAP (PC)	SPREAD (PC)	SecEnr (PC)	EHII2 (PC)
1990	-	-	9.14 (16.6)	-	-	-	22.46 (96.5)	-	-
1991	98.6 (71.3)	15.49 (67.7)	7.99 (12.8)	-	-	-	20.55 (96.4)	-	-
1992	91.42 (65.1)	6.02 (62.2)	6.51 (6.4)	-	-	-	17.9 (96.1)	-	-
1993	83.26 (60.9)	-3.86 (55.3)	6.12 (4.2)	-	-	-	14.96 (93.6)	-	-
1994	77.64 (57.4)	-10.25 (49.6)	6.44 (6.2)	-	-	-	12.65 (90)	-	-
1995	72.16 (52.6)	-16.49 (40.4)	6.1 (3.9)	-	-	-	9.41 (80.4)	-	-
1996	67.08 (47.4)	-22.19 (29.6)	6.12 (4)	-	12.2 (43.6)	-	-	-	-
1997	62.08 (43.4)	-27.56 (24.5)	6.17 (4.4)	-	10.72 (36.4)	-	-	66.303 (74.1)	-
1998	56.81 (39.2)	-32.99 (19.3)	5.72 (3.3)	-	10.51 (35.5)	--	-	70.235 (80.9)	-
1999	53.66 (36)	-36.22 (17.6)	5.19 (2)	5.19 (7.8)	-	12.56 (26)	-	-	-

OMAN

Gross domestic savings, gross fixed capital formation and GDP per capita growth over time

Year	Investment climate indicators		
	GDS5MA	GFCF5MA	INVCLIMATE
1975	49 (98.2)	32.32 (89.1)	SI (90)
1976	48.93 (98.1)	33.02 (89.9)	SI (90.4)
1977	46.89 (97.6)	31.82 (88.1)	SI (85)
1978	45.85 (97)	29.19 (82.5)	SI (79.5)
1979	.45.32 (96.8)	26.48 (69.3)	SI (75.4)
1980	44.74 (96.6)	25.35 (64.4)	RX (75.8)
1981	45.45 (96.8)		
1982	44.72 (96.6)		
1983	43.3 (96.2)		
1984	39.48 (94.1)		
1985	38.8 (93.7)		
1986	35.79 (91.5)		
1987	33.26 (88.2)		
1988	32.25 (86.8)		
1989	31.46 (85.7)		
1990	29.33 (82.5)		
1991	28.84 (81.7)		
1992	28.17 (80.9)		
1993			
1994			
1995			
1996			
1997			
1998			
1999			

Source: World Bank Group, World Development Indicators (WDI) database.

Note: Yellow circles indicate gross domestic savings; red triangles, gross fixed capital formation; and green quadrants, GDP per capita growth (all observations are five-year moving averages). Variables and other technical details are explained in annex II; All indicators are assigned their percentile ranks in the sample. Percentile ranks are in parentheses next to the absolute value and are denoted in column headings as 'PC'; A hyphen (-) indicates that the item is not applicable.

OMAN

Demand side indicators

Year	GDP(PC)	GDPCAP(PC)	GDPCAPgr(PC)	GDPCAPVOL(PC)	ICRG(PC)	DEBT(PC)	GOV(PC)
1990	9 241 (50.7)	5 500.4 (83.1)	1.55 (44.2)	1.95 (27.1)	66.9 (63.8)	29.76 (32.9)	33.6 (97.1)
1991	9 872 (51.7)	5 555.4 (83.2)	1.02 (36.4)	1.83 (24.4)	69.5 (72.9)	29.31 (32)	33.1 (96.8)
1992	10 528.2 (52.8)	5 613.6 (83.3)	1.07 (37.1)	1.81 (23.7)	73.1 (85.9)	29.88 (33.2)	33.36 (96.9)
1993	11 132.4 (53.7)	5 631 (83.4)	0.31 (27.5)	0.53 (1.3)	74.6 (90.1)	31.79 (36.6)	-
1994	11 639.8 (54.1)	5 651.6 (83.5)	0.36 (28.1)	0.61 (2)	76 (92.3)	30.94 (35.3)	-
1995	12 167.2 (54.8)	5 704.8 (83.7)	0.94 (35.3)	0.82 (4.6)	76.3 (92.7)	29.04 (31.7)	-
1996	12 616.4 (55.5)	5 761.4 (83.7)	0.99 (36)	0.78 (3.8)	76.4 (93)	28.68 (31)	-
1997	12 978.8 (56)	5 784.8 (83.8)	0.42 (28.9)	1.66 (20.1)	75.6 (91.9)	27.29 (29.6)	-
1998	13 406.4 (56.5)	5 833 (83.9)	0.85 (34.3)	1.89 (25.2)	75.96 (92.2)	24.86 (27.1)	-
1999	-	-	-	-	76.82 (93.6)	-	-

Supply side indicators

Year	FTS(PC)	FTSyc(PC)	MerchX (PC)	MerchXwO (PC)	MANU (PC)	MARKETCAP (PC)	SPREAD (PC)	SecEnr (PC)	EHII2 (PC)
1990	-	-	58.14 (88.5)	6.83 (15.3)	4.17 (3.1)	-	1.99 (8.6)	-	61.44 (97.3)
1991	-	-	57.65 (88.4)	7.66 (22.5)	-	-	2.49 (11.3)	-	61.44 (97.3)
1992	87.87 (62.7)	-14.99 (43.7)	55.94 (87.9)	8.71 (25.2)	-	-	3.06 (15)	49.056 (47.9)	61.44 (97.3)
1993	-	-	51.77 (86)	9.7 (28.7)	-	-	3.36 (18.7)	-	61.44 (97.3)
1994	-	-	52.21 (86.5)	10.55 (32.8)	-	13.59 (29)	3.34 (18.4)	-	59.84 (96.3)
1995	-	-	52 (86.3)	11.29 (36.8)	-	20.69 (46)	3.15 (15.4)	-	57.99 (96)
1996	-	-	49.72 (85.3)	11.62 (38.1)	-	24.98 (49.6)	2.62 (11.8)	-	55.79 (94.8)
1997	-	-	49.7 (85.3)	11.57 (37.9)	-	27.44 (53)	2.21 (9.7)	56.936 (60.7)	54.24 (94.7)
1998	-	-	53.24 (86.7)	11.8 (39.5)	-	27.67 (53.6)	2.13 (9.2)	57.655 (62.6)	51.97 (93.4)
1999	-	-	-	-	-	-	2.6 (11.8)	58.541 (64.5)	51.18 (92)

QATAR

Demand side indicators

Year	GDP(PC)	GDPCAP(PC)	GDPCAPgr(PC)	GDPCAPVOL(PC)	ICRG(PC)	DEBT(PC)	GOV(PC)
1990	-	-	-	-	62.3 (48.8)	-	-
1991	-	-	-	--	66.3 (61.6)	-	-
1992	-	-	-	-	70.2 (75.5)	-	-
1993	-	-	-	-	72.3 (82.7)	-	-
1994	-	-	-	-	73.7 (87.4)	-	-
1995	-	-	-	-	73.05 (85.6)	-	-
1996	-	-	-	-	71.8 (80.9)	-	-
1997	-	-	-	-	69.76 (73.7)	-	-
1998	-	-	-	-	69.26 (71.8)	-	-
1999	-	-	-	-	69.12 (70.7)	-	-

Supply side indicators

Year	FTS(PC)	FTSyc(PC)	MerchX (PC)	MerchXwO (PC)	MANU (PC)	MARKETCAP (PC)	SPREAD (PC)	SecEnr (PC)	EHII2 (PC)
1990	-	-	-	-	-	-	3.48 (19.8)	67.136 (74.9)	68.66 (99)
1991	-	-	-	-	-	-	3.4 (19.2)	66.239 (73.8)	64 (99)
1992	-	-	-	-	-	-	3.51 (20.1)	70.127 (80.3)	60.55 (96.5)
1993	-	-	-	-	-	-	-	69.4 (79.2)	57.42 (96)
1994	-	-	-	-	-	-	-	-	54.41 (94.8)
1995	-	-	-	-	-	-	-	-	51.97 (93.4)
1996	-	-	-	-	-	-	-	-	52.5 (94.1)
1997	-	-	-	-	-	-	-	69.442 (79.5)	52.44 (94.1)
1998	-	-	-	-	-	-	-	78.005 (88.2)	52.04 (93.5)
1999	-	-	-	-	-	-	-	-	52.11 (93.7)

Source: World Bank Group, World Development Indicators (WDI) database.

All indicators are assigned their percentile ranks in the sample. Percentile ranks are in parentheses next to the absolute value and are denoted in column headings as 'PC';
A hyphen (-) indicates that the item is not applicable.

SAUDI ARABIA

Gross domestic savings, gross fixed capital formation and GDP per capita growth over time

Year	Investment climate indicators		
	GDS5MA	GFCF5MA	INVCLIMATE
1975	68.38 (99.7)	19.23 (29.8)	RX (100)
1976	61.08 (99.3)	23.68 (55.5)	RX (96.5)
1977	56.62 (99.1)	26.18 (67.9)	RX (93.1)
1978	55.48 (99)	26.19 (68)	RX (91.9)
1979	53.11 (98.8)	25.86 (66.8)	RX (89.6)
1980	49.4 (98.4)	25.49 (65)	RX (87.3)
1981	45.55 (97)	25.25 (63.9)	RX (77)
1982	38.92 (93.8)	25.71 (65.9)	SI (49.5)
1983	29.09 (82)	26.48 (69.3)	AVG (NA)
1984	20.62 (60)	26.7 (71)	AVG (NA)
1985	15.68 (38.3)	25.87 (66.9)	RM (20)
1986	14.19 (30.8)	23.96 (57.7)	RM (33.4)
1987	14.61 (32.6)	22.35 (46.8)	VC (31.7)
1988	17.91 (49)	21.26 (40.3)	VC (6.9)
1989	21 (61.8)	20.29 (35.8)	AVG (NA)
1990	24.23 (73.1)	19.63 (32.2)	AVG (NA)
1991	26.35 (77.9)	20.08 (34.5)	AVG (NA)
1992	28.32 (81.1)	19.93 (33.8)	AVG (NA)
1993	29.18 (82.2)	20.08 (34.5)	RX (5.7)
1994	30.59 (83.9)	19.64 (32.4)	RX (29.8)
1995	31.33 (85.5)	19.11 (29.2)	RX (39)
1996	30.95 (84.7)	18.8 (27.4)	RX (36.7)
1997	31.06 (84.9)	18.98 (28.4)	RX (35.6)
1998	31.77 (86.3)	18.56 (25.8)	RX (43.6)
1999	32.72 (87.4)	18.7 (27.1)	RX (47.1)

Source: World Bank Group, World Development Indicators (WDI) database.

Note: Yellow circles indicate gross domestic savings; red triangles, gross fixed capital formation; and green quadrants, GDP per capita growth (all observations are five-year moving averages). Variables and other technical details are explained in annex II; All indicators are assigned their percentile ranks in the sample. Percentile ranks are in parentheses next to the absolute value and are denoted in column headings as 'PC'; A hyphen (-) indicates that the item is not applicable.

SAUDI ARABIA

Demand side indicators

Year	GDP(PC)	GDPCAP(PC)	GDPCAPgr(PC)	GDPCAPVOL(PC)	ICRG(PC)	DEBT(PC)	GOV(PC)
1990	114 035.8 (88.4)	7 254.6 (87.6)	1.7 (46.1)	4.38 (68)	64.9 (56.9)	-	33.1 (96.8)
1991	118 738.8 (88.6)	7 290 (87.9)	0.58 (30.8)	4.85 (72.9)	68.4 (69.3)	-	32.02 (96.1)
1992	123 526.4 (89)	7 358 (88.3)	1.05 (36.7)	4.33 (67)	70.6 (76.5)	-	31.12 (95.3)
1993	126 641.6 (89.2)	7 341.6 (88.2)	-0.16 (23.5)	4.18 (65.9)	73.3 (86.3)	-	30.13 (94.6)
1994	127 761 (89.2)	7 207.2 (87.3)	-1.83 (12.3)	1.04 (7.5)	74.4 (89.3)	-	27.56 (91.8)
1995	128 708.4 (89.3)	7 071 (86.8)	-1.86 (12.1)	0.98 (6.4)	74.1 (88.5)	-	26.34 (90.6)
1996	130 277.8 (89.5)	6 971.2 (86.7)	-1.39 (15)	0.7 (3)	73.4 (86.8)	-	26.26 (90.2)
1997	131 513.8 (89.7)	6 857.4 (86.2)	-1.63 (13.7)	1.1 (8.4)	72.46 (83.2)	-	26.05 (90.2)
1998	133 931.6 (89.9)	6 803.6 (86)	-0.77 (19.2)	1.96 (27.3)	72.96 (85.3)	-	26.13 (90.4)
1999	136 329 (89.9)	6 739.4 (85.8)	-0.93 (17.8)	2.04 (28.7)	73.82 (88.2)	-	26.63 (91.2)

Supply side indicators

Year	FTS(PC)	FTSyc(PC)	MerchX (PC)	MerchXwO (PC)	MANU (PC)	MARKETCAP (PC)	SPREAD (PC)	SecEnr (PC)	EHII2 (PC)
1990	80.9 (59.7)	-27.03 (24.8)	39.35 (78.4)	4.2 (4.8)	8.19 (21.9)	-	-	31.168 (19.8)	-
1991	81.16 (59.9)	-26.87 (25)	40.28 (78.9)	3.86 (4.2)	8.17 (21.8)	-	-	32.04 (20.9)	-
1992	79.84 (59.2)	-28.37 (23.5)	40.42 (79.1)	3.61 (3.7)	8.31 (22.6)	-	-	33.984 (22.8)	-
1993	78.22 (58)	-29.95 (21.8)	38.99 (78.1)	3.81 (4.1)	-	38.84 (71.8)	-	36.6 (27.5)	-
1994	74.43 (54.6)	-33.37 (18.9)	39.45 (78.4)	4.15 (4.6)	-	36.48 (69.6)	-	-	-
1995	70.65 (51.2)	-36.77 (17.5)	39.58 (78.6)	-	-	34.76 (66)	-	47.632 (46.3)	-
1996	66.43 (46.5)	-40.71 (14.9)	37.92 (77.5)	-	-	31.68 (60)	-	42.482 (37.6)	-
1997	64.3 (45)	-42.52 (13.7)	37.94 (77.6)	-	-	32.74 (63)	-	-	-
1998	63.15 (44.2)	-43.51 (13.3)	39.98 (78.8)	-	-	33.46 (64.5)	-	-	-
1999	63.02 (44)	-43.45 (13.4)	39.18 (78.2)	-	-	35.5 (67.8)	-	-	-

39

SYRIAN ARAB REPUBLIC

Gross domestic savings, gross fixed capital formation and GDP per capita growth over time

	Investment climate indicators		
Year	GDS5MA	GFCF5MA	INVCLIMATE
1975	14.95 (34.1)	27.75 (76.5)	RM (33.1)
1976	15.58 (37.5)	29.79 (84.4)	RM (37)
1977	14.36 (31.6)	31.25 (87.1)	RM (45.6)
1978	13.94 (30)	31.79 (88)	RM (51)
1979	11.66 (22.4)	30.03 (84.9)	RM (57)
1980	11.45 (21.8)	27.48 (75.2)	RM (53.1)
1981	11.23 (21)	26.65 (70.6)	RM (53.4)
1982	11.78 (22.7)	26.13 (67.8)	RM (48.3)
1983	11.9 (23.1)	25.32 (64.2)	RM (46.5)
1984	12.99 (27.2)	25.11 (63.1)	RM (41.1)
1985	11.35 (21.3)	23.94 (57.6)	RM (50.7)
1986	10.14 (18.4)	21.87 (44.5)	VC (61.9)
1987	9.86 (17.2)	20.2 (35.3)	VC (66.6)
1988	10.71 (20)	18.41 (25)	VC (65)
1989	10.23 (18.5)	17.23 (18.4)	VC (70.1)
1990	11.38 (21.5)	17.96 (22.1)	VC (61.7)
1991	12.84 (26.8)	20.16 (34.9)	VC (48.6)
1992	13.92 (30)	22.72 (50.1)	VC (37.6)
1993	14.59 (32.5)	24.86 (61.7)	RM (29.8)
1994	16.06 (40.2)	26.04 (67.6)	RM (17.9)
1995	17.64 (47.4)	25.63 (65.5)	RM (4.1)
1996	19.39 (55.5)	24.77 (61.1)	AVG (-)
1997	20.15 (58.4)	22.74 (50.3)	AVG (-)
1998	21.53 (63.9)	21.12 (39.8)	AVG (-)
1999	23.73 (71.3)	20.57 (37.2)	AVG (-)

Source: World Bank Group, World Development Indicators (WDI) database.

Note: Yellow circles indicate gross domestic savings; red triangles, gross fixed capital formation; and green quadrants, GDP per capita growth (all observations are five-year moving averages).
Variables and other technical details are explained in annex II; All indicators are assigned their percentile ranks in the sample. Percentile ranks are in parentheses next to the absolute value and are denoted in column headings as 'PC'; A hyphen (-) indicates that the item is not applicable.

40

SYRIAN ARAB REPUBLIC

Demand side indicators

Year	GDP(PC)	GDPCAP(PC)	GDPCAPgr(PC)	GDPCAPVOL(PC)	ICRG(PC)	DEBT(PC)	GOV(PC)
1990	8 167 (49)	672.8 (18.6)	3.21 (67)	8.88 (94)	48.7 (14.4)	-	14.65 (51.8)
1991	8 582.6 (49.7)	682.8 (19)	1.66 (46)	8.14 (92.3)	54.4 (25.4)	-	14.73 (52)
1992	9 293.6 (50.9)	716 (20.6)	4.91 (85.1)	2.95 (48.8)	59.4 (38.9)	-	14.21 (50.4)
1993	10 018.2 (51.9)	747.8 (21.7)	4.58 (83)	3.14 (51.3)	63.1 (51.5)	-	14.03 (49.5)
1994	10 720.2 (53.1)	776.6 (22.1)	4.01 (77.6)	3.43 (55.8)	65.4 (58.7)	-	13.33 (45.8)
1995	11 239 (53.7)	790.8 (22.6)	1.87 (49.3)	1.87 (25)	67.1 (65.2)	-	12.73 (42.4)
1996	11 843.4 (54.4)	810 (23.1)	2.47 (57.5)	2.31 (35.5)	67.9 (67.3)	-	12.16 (39.1)
1997	12 242.4 (55)	815.4 (23.5)	0.73 (32.6)	3.55 (57.4)	68.36 (69.1)	-	11.52 (34.8)
1998	12 532.8 (55.3)	814 (23.4)	-0.14 (23.7)	3.54 (57.3)	68.62 (69.7)	-	11.09 (32.1)
1999	12 795 (55.6)	810.4 (23.1)	-0.39 (21.8)	3.43 (55.9)	69.62 (73.5)	-	10.9 (31)

Supply side indicators

Year	FTS(PC)	FTSyc(PC)	MerchX (PC)	MerchXwO (PC)	MANU (PC)	MARKETCAP (PC)	SPREAD (PC)	SecEnr (PC)	EHII2 (PC)
1990	54.94 (37.4)	-5.98 (53.3)	43.44 (81.7)	-	-	-	5 (40.1)	45.827 (42.7)	41.33 (29.5)
1991	59.96 (41.9)	-1.25 (57.7)	45.69 (82.5)	-	-	-	5 (40.1)	44.58 (40)	41.31 (29.4)
1992	64.78 (45.6)	2.63 (59.7)	41.34 (80.2)	-	15.87 (58.1)	-	5 (40.1)	43.87 (39.5)	41.57 (30.6)
1993	67.31 (47.6)	4.3 (60.6)	34.92 (75.6)	-	14.56 (52)	-	5 (40.1)	42 (36.7)	42.83 (40.9)
1994	70 (50.4)	6.24 (62.4)	32.28 (72.9)	-	15.3 (55.1)	-	5 (40.1)	39.953 (33.5)	44.86 (57.6)
1995	70.47 (51.1)	6.36 (62.6)	31.34 (72)	-	17.52 (67.7)	-	5 (40.1)	38.787 (31)	46.78 (73.4)
1996	69.37 (49.8)	4.78 (61.2)	28.86 (67.4)	-	19.3 (77)	-	5 (40.1)	38.088 (30.2)	48.02 (84.1)
1997	67.11 (47.5)	2.39 (59.6)	27.98 (66.2)	9.89 (29.2)	21.99 (83.1)	-	5 (40.1)	38.377 (30.5)	49.19 (89.3)
1998	66.99 (47.2)	2.3 (59.5)	28.14 (66.6)	9.06 (26.3)	24.34 (89.6)	-	5 (40.1)	37.589 (28.8)	47.63 (80.6)
1999	66.79 (46.9)	2.19 (59.5)	27.47 (65.4)	-	25.02 (90.8)	-	5 (40.1)	-	45.51 (61.8)

Year	Investment climate indicators			Gross domestic savings, gross fixed capital formation and GDP per capita growth over time
	GDS5MA	GFCF5MA	INVCLIMATE	
1975	76.25 (100)			
1976	74.32 (99.9)			
1977	71.23 (99.8)	35.53 (93.4)	SI (100)	
1978	70.41 (99.8)	34.89 (92.5)	SI (99.5)	
1979	67.58 (99.6)	33.43 (90.5)	SI (99)	
1980	64.96 (99.6)	32.02 (88.5)	SI (98.6)	
1981	62.78 (99.5)	29.68 (84)	SI (98.1)	
1982	60.28 (99.3)	28.26 (78.8)	SI (97.7)	
1983	56.51 (99)	27.7 (76.3)	SI (96.8)	
1984	51.82 (98.8)	28.51 (80.4)	SI (93.1)	
1985	48.64 (98)	27.38 (74.7)	SI (86.8)	
1986	44.5 (96.5)	25.98 (67.4)	SI (73.6)	
1987	40.92 (95.2)	24.69 (60.5)	RX (72.4)	
1988	39.37 (94)	23.6 (55.1)	RX (68.9)	
1989	39.98 (94.4)	21.81 (44)	RX (70.1)	
1990	38.98 (93.9)	21.69 (43.2)	RX (67.8)	
1991	38.72 (93.5)	21.45 (41.8)	RX (66.6)	
1992	36.24 (92.1)	21.82 (44.1)	RX (63.2)	

Source: World Bank Group, World Development Indicators (WDI) database.

Note: Yellow circles indicate gross domestic savings; red triangles, gross fixed capital formation; and green quadrants, GDP per capita growth (all observations are five-year moving averages).

Variables and other technical details are explained in annex II;
All indicators are assigned their percentile ranks in the sample. Percentile ranks are in parentheses next to the absolute value and are denoted in column headings as 'PC';
A hyphen (-) indicates that the item is not applicable.

United Arab Emirates

Demand side indicators

Year	GDP(PC)	GDPCAP(PC)	GDPCAPgr(PC)	GDPCAPVOL(PC)	ICRG(PC)	DEBT(PC)	GOV(PC)
1990	35 850.4 (68.9)	19 382 (97.9)	-0.42 (21.5)	7.76 (90.5)	61.8 (46.9)	-	18.21 (69.3)
1991	37 943.6 (70)	19 280.8 (97.8)	-0.33 (22.3)	7.64 (90.2)	65.5 (59)	-	17.45 (65.4)
1992	39 425 (70.8)	18 948.2 (97.7)	-1.6 (13.9)	6.8 (86.9)	69.1 (70.5)	-	17.05 (63.7)
1993	40 245.6 (71.1)	18 407.6 (97.6)	-2.61 (9.3)	5.02 (74.9)	71.7 (80.6)	-	-
1994	41 910.4 (72.1)	18 383.6 (97.5)	-0.03 (24.3)	4.81 (72.5)	74.2 (88.6)	-	-
1995	43 568.2 (73)	18 289.4 (97.5)	-0.4 (21.6)	4.95 (74.1)	75.5 (91.8)	-	-
1996	44 753.8 (73.5)	18 082.8 (97.4)	-1.04 (17.1)	6.15 (83.3)	76.35 (92.9)	-	-
1997	-	-	-	-	77.15 (93.8)	-	-
1998	-	-	-	-	78.35 (95.1)	-	-
1999	-	-	-	-	79.65 (96.9)	-	-

Supply side indicators

Year	FTS(PC)	FTSyc(PC)	MerchX (PC)	MerchXwO (PC)	MANU (PC)	MARKETCAP (PC)	SPREAD (PC)	SecEnr (PC)	EHII2 (PC)
1990	108.89 (77.5)	-18.47 (36.3)	65.75 (91.3)	62.33 (93.6)	8.15 (21.8)	-	-	59.188 (66.2)	45.71 (64.2)
1991	114.11 (80)	-13.14 (46.5)	66.35 (91.5)	62.9 (93.8)	8.01 (21)	-	-	61.242 (67.8)	45.71 (64.2)
1992	119.63 (82.1)	-7.28 (52.6)	66.95 (91.6)	-	-	-	-	64.249 (71.6)	45.71 (64.2)
1993	-	-	65.68 (91.2)	-	-	-	-	68.4 (77.3)	45.71 (64.2)
1994	-	-	63.14 (90.4)	-	-	-	-	71.12 (83.3)	45.71 (64.2)
1995	-	-	63.02 (90.2)	-	-	-	-	-	45.71 (64.2)
1996	-	-	64.31 (90.9)	-	-	-	-	70.647 (82.5)	45.71 (64.2)
1997	-	-	-	-	-	-	-	69.144 (79)	45.71 (64.2)
1998	-	-	-	-	-	-	-	68.018 (76.5)	45.71 (64.2)
1999	--	-	-	-	-	-	-	67.46 (75.7)	45.71 (64.2)

WEST BANK AND GAZA STRIP

	Investment climate indicators		
Year	GDS5MA	GFCF5MA	INVCLIMATE
1996	-14.86 (1.5)	34.35 (91.6)	RM (94.6)
1997	-17.62 (0.9)	36.05 (94.2)	RM (95.2)
1998	-20.93 (0.8)	35.59 (93.6)	RM (96.1)
1999	-	-	-

Gross domestic savings, gross fixed capital formation and GDP per capita growth over time

Source: World Bank Group, World Development Indicators (WDI) database.

Note: Yellow circles indicate gross domestic savings; red triangles, gross fixed capital formation; and green quadrants, GDP per capita growth (all observations are five-year moving averages).

Variables and other technical details are explained in annex II;

All indicators are assigned their percentile ranks in the sample. Percentile ranks are in parentheses next to the absolute value and are denoted in column headings as 'PC';

A hyphen (-) indicates that the item is not applicable.

WEST BANK AND GAZA STRIP

Demand side indicators

Year	GDP(PC)	GDPCAP(PC)	GDPCAPgr(PC)	GDPCAPVOL(PC)	ICRG(PC)	DEBT(PC)	GOV(PC)
1990	-	-	-	-	-	-	-
1991	-	-	-	-	-	-	-
1992	-	-	-	-	-	-	-
1993	-	-	-	-	-	-	-
1994	-	-	-	-	-	-	-
1995	-	-	-	-	-	-	-
1996	3 732.8 (34.6)	1 486.8 (42.2)	-	-	-	-	20.56 (78.5)
1997	3 861.8 (35)	1 471.8 (41.7)	-0.89 (18.3)	4.36 (67.4)	-	-	21.91 (81.9)
1998	3 953.6 (35.3)	1 445 (40.8)	-1.71 (13.4)	5.76 (81.1)	-	-	24.52 (87.9)
1999	3 943.2 (35.2)	1 388.4 (39.4)	-3.98 (5.6)	8.51 (93.3)	-	-	-

Supply side indicators

Year	FTS(PC)	FTSyc(PC)	MerchX (PC)	MerchXwO (PC)	MANU (PC)	MARKETCAP (PC)	SPREAD (PC)	SecEnr (PC)	EHII2 (PC)
1990	-	-	-	-	-	-	-	-	-
1991	-	-	-	-	-	-	-	-	-
1992	-	-	-	-	-	-	-	-	-
1993	-	-	-	-	-	-	-	-	-
1994	-	-	-	-	-	-	-	-	-
1995	-	-	-	-	-	-	-	-	-
1996	84.22 (61.2)	7.62 (63.4)	-	-	15.82 (57.4)	-	-	-	-
1997	87.88 (62.7)	11.48 (65.2)	-	-	16.39 (60.8)	-	-	-	-
1998	89.45 (63.9)	13.42 (66.4)	-	-	15.96 (58.4)	-	-	-	-
1999	-	-	-	-	-	-	-	-	16.54 (36.9)

45

YEMEN

Gross domestic savings, gross fixed capital formation and GDP per capita growth over time

Year	Investment climate indicators		
	GDS5MA	GFCF5MA	INVCLIMATE
1992	-1.45 (4.1)	16.43 (14.5)	VC (98.2)
1993	-0.29 (4.3)	18.17 (23.5)	VC (97.3)
1994	4.07 (8)	19.65 (32.5)	VC (88.8)
1995	8.59 (14.4)	19.95 (34)	VC (72)
1996	14.36 (31.6)	22.7 (50)	VC (33.1)
1997	15.96 (39.7)	23.46 (54.4)	RM (17.3)
1998	18.7 (52.7)	23.26 (53.6)	AVG (NA)
1999	19.7 (56.6)	22.91 (51.3)	AVG (NA)

Source: World Bank Group, World Development Indicators (WDI) database.

Note: Yellow circles indicate gross domestic savings; red triangles, gross fixed capital formation; and green quadrants, GDP per capita growth (all observations are five-year moving averages).

Variables and other technical details are explained in annex II;

All indicators are assigned their percentile ranks in the sample. Percentile ranks are in parentheses next to the absolute value and are denoted in column headings as 'PC';

A hyphen (-) indicates that the item is not applicable.

YEMEN

Demand side indicators

Year	GDP(PC)	FTSyc(PC)	GDPCAP(PC)	GDPCAPgr(PC)	GDPCAPVOL(PC)	ICRG(PC)	DEBT(PC)	GOV(PC)
1990	-	-	-	-	-	-	-	-
1991	-	-	-	-	-	-	-	-
1992	3 520.6 (33.9)	-	258.6 (3.9)	-	-	53.9 (23.4)	-	18.76 (71.8)
1993	3 721.6 (34.5)	-	260 (4)	0.68 (32)	6.9 (87.3)	56.8 (31.5)	-	18.13 (69)
1994	3 961 (35.3)	-	268.2 (4.4)	3.24 (67.5)	3.74 (60.5)	61.2 (44.1)	-	16.94 (62.8)
1995	4 217.2 (35.9)	-	277 (4.8)	3.26 (67.7)	3.75 (60.7)	62.4 (49.1)	-	15.68 (56.6)
1996	4 507 (37)	-	287.4 (5.5)	3.81 (75.3)	3.48 (56.4)	63.4 (52.3)	-	14.76 (52.3)
1997	4 809.2 (38.2)	-	298.4 (6)	4 (77.1)	3.16 (51.6)	63.76 (52.8)	-	13.69 (47.8)
1998	5 069.8 (39.3)	-	305.8 (6.3)	2.58 (58.9)	1.95 (27.1)	63.56 (52.5)	-	13.43 (46.4)
1999	5 313.6 (40.6)	-	311.6 (6.6)	1.97 (50.6)	2.22 (33.2)	63.82 (53.2)	-	13.62 (47.3)

Supply side indicators

Year	FTS(PC)	MerchX (PC)	MerchXwO (PC)	MANU (PC)	MARKETCAP (PC)	SPREAD (PC)	SecEnr (PC)	EHI2 (PC)
1975	-	-	-	-	-	-	-	51.02 (91.8)
1976	-	-	-	-	-	-	-	52.22 (93.8)
1977	-	-	-	-	-	-	-	52.98 (94.3)
1978	-	-	-	-	-	-	-	50.76 (91.1)
1979	-	-	-	-	-	-	-	48.64 (87.4)
1980	-	-	-	-	-	-	-	46.28 (70.2)
1981	-	-	-	-	-	-	-	44.3 (54.6)
1982	-	-	-	-	-	-	-	42.53 (39)
1983	-	-	-	-	-	-	-	42.98 (43)
1984	-	-	-	-	-	-	-	43.08 (44.3)
1985	-	-	-	-	-	-	-	43.01 (43.5)
1986	-	-	-	-	-	-	-	42.62 (39.6)
1987	-	-	-	-	-	-	-	42.27 (36.3)
1988	-	-	-	-	-	-	-	42.28 (36.9)
1989	-	-	-	-	-	-	-	42.1 (34.2)

Supply side indicators

Year	FTS(PC)	FTSyc(PC)	MerchX (PC)	MerchXwO (PC)	MANU (PC)	MARKETCAP (PC)	SPREAD (PC)	SecEnr (PC)	EHI12 (PC)
1990	-	-	-	-	-	-	-	-	42.12 (34.5)
1991	-	-	-	-	-	-	-	-	42.12 (34.5)
1992	71.57 (51.9)	29.55 (78.6)	23.18 (55.9)	-	11.19 (38.8)	-	-	-	42.12 (34.5)
1993	86.45 (62.1)	44.33 (85.3)	27.35 (65.3)	-	12.16 (43.4)	-	-	-	42.12 (34.5)
1994	94.88 (68.7)	52.14 (88.1)	34.43 (75.2)	-	12.31 (43.8)	-	-	-	42.12 (34.5)
1995	96.53 (70.4)	53.15 (88.3)	40.46 (79.2)	-	12.16 (43.4)	-	-	-	42.12 (34.5)
1996	92.82 (66.3)	48.72 (86.9)	41.01 (79.9)	-	11.79 (41.6)	-	-	-	42.12 (34.5)
1997	85.57 (61.8)	40.72 (84.1)	44.31 (82.2)	-	10.64 (36.2)	-	-	-	42.12 (34.5)
1998	79.74 (59.1)	34.41 (81.4)	48.23 (84.5)	-	9.1 (26.7)	-	6.01 (54.7)	36.98 (28)	42.12 (34.5)
1999	76.49 (56.2)	30.79 (79.2)	46.33 (83)	-	8.3 (22.5)	-	5.37 (46.4)	-	42.12 (34.5)